Short Plays

KEITH DEWHURST was born in 1931 and worked in a cotton mill and as a journalist before becoming a playwright. Three of his seventeen stage plays were premiered at the Royal Court Theatre and six at the National Theatre. He has written two movies, eighteen TV plays and episodes for many series, including the original 'Z-Cars'.

Short Plays

KEITH DEWHURST

GREENHEART PRESS

First published in Great Britain 2024
by Greenheart Press (Greenheart Press Plays)
25 Douglas Avenue, Whitstable, Kent CT5 1RT

Copyright © Keith Dewhurst 2024

Keith Dewhurst has asserted his moral right to be identified as author of this Work in accordance with sections 77 and 78 of the Copyright, Designs and Patents Act 1988

All rights reserved. No part of this work may be reproduced, stored in a retrieval system, or transmitted, in any form or by any means, electronic, mechanical, photocopying, recording otherwise, without the prior written permission of the publisher.

A CIP catalogue record for this book is available from the British Library

ISBN 978-0-9571829-8-1

Caution

All rights whatsoever in this play are strictly reserved. Application for professional or amateur performing rights should be made before rehearsals begin to Alexandra Cann Representation, Box 116, 4 Montpelier Street, London SW7 1EE.
Email alex@alexandracann.co.uk
No performance may be given unless a licence has been obtained.

Produced by The Choir Press
Cover Design by Paul Baker of A Stones Throw

For Millicent, Henry and Alexander

Also by Keith Dewhurst

PLAYS
Rafferty's Chant in 'Plays of the Year'
Lark Rise to Candleford
War Plays (Corunna!, The World Turned Upside Down, The Bomb in Brewery Street)
Don Quixote
Black Snow
Philoctetes (translation)

TELEVISION
Running Milligan in 'Z-Cars'
Last Bus in 'Scene'

NOVELS
Captain of the Sands
McSullivan's Beach
The History of Polly Bowler
Dancing Bear

NOVELLAS
Autumnia
Venice Three

THEATRE MEMOIR
Impossible Plays (with Jack Shepherd)

FOOTBALL
When You Put on a Red Shirt: Memories of Matt Busby, Jimmy Murphy and Manchester United
Underdogs: The Unlikely Story of Football's First F.A. Cup Heroes

Foreword

Sir George Buck, Master of the Revels and censor of plays, needed to know who had written a very obscure play published in 1599. So, bumping into Shakespeare, he asked *him*. Buck received a confident reply, including who had played the lead.

Talking to Keith Dewhurst in his ninety-second year (2023), I am constantly reminded of this incident, because there seems to be no event in the British theatre of the last seventy years that Dewhurst cannot connect with instantly through his own experience and amazing memory. The reason is the same as with Shakespeare: Dewhurst's whole life has been immersed to the ink-stained fingertips, so to speak, in the craft of writing plays and the life of the theatre.

But there is a more important, underlying consonance. Dewhurst believes there have been two periods of great dramatic writing in the British theatre – the Elizabethan-Jacobean and the English Revival of roughly 1956-1990. The bulk of his own dramatic writing, whether television plays, radio plays, or plays for the Royal Court and National Theatre, falls within the Revival. He is one of its central surviving writers, having worked closely with such uncompromising directors as Bill Bryden (*Pirates*, *The World Turned Upside Down*, *Lark Rise*, *Don Quixote*) and William Gaskill (*Black Snow*). Moreover, he feels that it is precisely a lack of rigour, both in writing and directing, that lies behind the decline of this second great period of British theatre. It is long over. As he said to me in a recent interview, 'it betrayed its own repertoire'; it became a theatre of 'spectacle and safely middlebrow content'; we are in a situation where 'writers are no longer at the vanguard of the conversation' and directors 'behave as though they invented something completely new'; one in which 'a morally good (by its own definition) opinion is all you need'.

The last new play by Keith Dewhurst to be performed in a theatre was *King Arthur* at the Arcola Theatre in 2006, when he was seventy-five. But he considers himself 'a slow developer; I got better at writing as the whole situation got worse!'. In this volume of four stage plays completed by Dewhurst since 2006, you will find that he himself has lost none of the power, originality and rigorous probing of reality that marked the second great period of British dramatic writing.

Spoilers aside here, *Sam's Father* and *Hannah Vine* cry out to be performed as a whole-evening double bill, as they explore two sides of the same phenomenon, which Dewhurst considers 'a kind of key subject', namely the Feminised modern woman. The heroine of the first, Norah, proclaims 'I hate lies', yet she lies compulsively (and her wealth as a TV producer is partly built on cooking the books). She and David feel a strong personal and sexual attraction, but it is all manipulated by her decision to make him 'the father of my baby' – not *their* baby, because she insists he sign a contract that when she is pregnant he will disappear from her life, never reveal his paternity, and she will tell their son (Sam) that his father is dead. 'I wanted a child but I didn't want a man.' The story beneath her lies and ideology is one of ruthless control in the name of 'a woman's right', including ending her life in a Swiss clinic 'on my own terms'. It is an eviscerating play – and a magnificent role for a female actor – but the completely credible manner in which life hits back, partly through the values of a younger generation, makes for a breathtaking finale and will put fresh hope into you. This is modern tragedy at its best (*Medea* is referenced).

'I'm not caught up in feminism. I mean, I know it's true' says the pulp biographer Barbara as she embarks on interviewing Delamere, a Cambridge English don whose critical thinking had a formative influence on his student Hannah Vine, a celebrated feminist. As Vine subversively predicted, 'political correctness has so constricted the rules of debate that it is impossible to discuss anything', Delamere tells Barbara, then sows doubts in her amoral mind. 'What do you think it would be like, a world with which women were satisfied?' It transpires that Hannah Vine was cancelled and committed suicide after raising the subject of sexual and maternal *instinct* in women's lives during a TV interview. 'Instinctive relationships were, she thought, under-discussed by feminists: mothers and daughters, mothers and sons – ', Delamere explains. Both Vine and her biographer mothered their children from casual sex. 'Love, Miss Babs, is a subject addressed more by my dead poets than your feminist writers. Why is that, do you think?' Nevertheless, Barbara succeeds in extracting from Delamere that he was Vine's lover, and Vine's widowed daughter appears, who has in effect been adopted by him. Dewhurst's gradual revelation of the facts of Vine's life and death is masterly, and again he achieves a totally unexpected ending. Delamere is a part for a virtuoso actor, but the two female roles are just as forceful and spark off each other irresistibly. Again, the play is about character – emotion – instinct – biology – intellect – soul – rather than 'opinion'.

Dewhurst's first job after graduating from Cambridge in 1953 was yarn testing at a cotton mill, and yarn testing of another kind is what he is always doing in his plays. His plots are never predictable. He is always playing with chance and possibility. What is going to happen next? Expect the unexpected. After all, a play is *play*: that is what draws us in, and as Schiller said, 'it is only when humans are playing that they are really free'. 'Most books', Dewhurst believes, 'are not like life, but like other books. Life is not how it's conventionally presented.'

This contrast is at the heart of the third play in the volume, *Steerforth in Italy*. Dewhurst plays with what might have happened if David Copperfield had gone to Italy to rescue Little Em'ly from her subjection to Steerforth, make her 'respectable', and take her home to 'Yarmouth and the chapel-goers ever after'. David in the play exceeds his own ingenuousness in Dickens's novel: he does not recognise Emily even when she is standing next to him as the successful singer La Peggotta and speaking fluent Italian! Steerforth, too, is entirely consistent with his received literary character, even when he has hilariously transformed himself into the woman Jemima, because he remains as flaky as in the novel: 'I can't think how many times in my life I was on the edge of being what I could be.' But Emily and Henri Beyle (Stendhal) live truly – a 'life not how it is conventionally presented'. Emily tells Henri: 'I left him [Steerforth]. Ran off. Had to.' Her 'seduction' by Steerforth actually released her libido. She planned and achieved around Steerforth a career as a *diva* with, reputedly, five lovers. As a psychologist and free individual, Emily is even the equal of Stendhal, who understands her and everyone else in the play completely (Dewhurst greatly admires his writing). It is a glorious comedy that cries out to be staged in a fast, epic style to make audiences think. 'In his memory,' says Henri of Copperfield, 'you are a fisher girl on a beach.' 'I never was the person he imagined,' replies Emily.

Of the last play in this volume, *St Boniface Gardens*, it could also be said that someone is shown as 'never the person we imagined': Karl Marx. He is in the last four months of his life, very ill, living in digs on the Isle of Wight at 1 St Boniface Gardens – a house Keith Dewhurst can see from his living room – toiling to finish *Das Kapital*, and being treated by a local doctor, James Williamson. Far from 'The Last Old Testament Prophet', as Dewhurst has called him in conversation, Marx is here a man consumed by fundamental *emotions*, especially guilt at his wife's death ('My struggle was the reef on which her life was wrecked'). His rich anger is not primarily political, but directed at his two sons-in-law, who are French socialist 'popinjays, windbags, scoundrels, posturers' completely unsuitable for his daughters Jenny and Laura. He struggles to understand why such 'progressive' men are frauds, and suspects that it is because his 'cause' is 'a new drug of religion' and would therefore always attract hypocrites. The play holds Marx at a threshold in his life, when he rejected Marxist 'revolutionary phrasemongers' like his sons-in-law and declared to Engels 'If one thing is certain, it is that I am not a Marxist'. Moreover, in her delightfully polite and playful interview with the 'prophet' (as she calls him), Dr Williamson's young wife draws Marx out on the subject of violent revolution – the very bone of contention with the young French socialists and, it seems, the stuff of Marx's actual nightmares ('I see violence and deaths. I am to blame'). *St Boniface Gardens* is a deeply human portrait based scrupulously on the facts and bursting with potential for its four actors. It is beautifully crafted.

But the same can be said of all the plays published here for the first time. Perhaps they have benefitted from being written in so-called retirement, as one imagines *The Tempest* benefitted. In my view they demonstrate beyond question that the long arc of Keith Dewhurst's career as a playwright is going to land safely on the other side of British theatre's present phase of self-inflicted aridity.

Patrick Miles January 2024
Literary consultant and translator to the National Theatre 1977-2015

Contents

SAM'S FATHER	1
HANNAH VINE	51
STEERFORTH IN ITALY	117
ST BONIFACE GARDENS	173

Sam's Father

CHARACTERS

Nora
David
Sam

Locations

Nora's house in North London

Nora's docklands duplex

Time

Then and Now

Scene One   **Nora's House in North London**   **Then**

*Nora is perhaps over thirty. **David** certainly forty-five.*

Nora   Tea? Coffee? Drink?

David: Whatever.

Nora   A drink then. Whisky? Brandy? Some awful watered-down Cointreau that I bought at La Jonquera?

David: What's La Jonquera?

Nora   It's a duty-free place in Spain.

David   Whisky.

Nora pours it.

Nora   Won't you take your coat off?

David   Would you mind awfully if I telephoned my wife?

Nora gives him the drink.

Nora   Go ahead.

David   Thank you.

David dials.

Nora leaves him to talk.

After a moment someone answers the phone.

David   Who's that? Winnie? It's dad. Is – Can you just tell – Okay. This is Space Admiral to Inter-Galactic Security. We have encountered a mysterious new energy field. Now please fetch your mother and – Yes. We are reporting as instructed to the High Priestess of the Temple of Puos Sllebpmac. Now go.

4 Sam's Father

David *waits. Then his wife answers.*

> Penny? How are you? Look, I will be a shade later than I thought. We can handle that, can't we? The meeting? It was fine.

Nora *returns.*

> Me? I'm fine apart from having to go through this Inter-Galactic Puos Sllebpmac stuff. Of course. I know. It's just a phase. Energy field? Well, that's it. There was someone at the meeting who owns a Paul Sandby drawing of the way the district looked in 1760. I've been invited in to look at it. Exactly. All systems go, as we say at Puos Sllebpmac. Home soon.

David *hangs up.*

> Thank you.

Nora	How many children do you have?
David	Three.
Nora	How old are they?
David	Thirteen, eleven and nine. Coming up to the rocky ride.
Nora	Boys?
David	A girl in the middle.
Nora	Very elegantly planned.
David	Thank you.
Nora	Is your wife able to work?
David	She's a consultant in the NHS.
Nora	What's Puos Sllebpmac?

David Kids' fantasies. It's Campbell's Soup backwards.

Nora You mean like Retipuj?

David What?

Nora The far side of Jupiter.

David Exactly. I suppose. Have I seen you before at the Residents' Association?

Nora Did somebody tell me that you're moving away?

David My wife's new job.

Nora Does it mean that you'll have to give up your shop?

David Sorry: but if we never met until today, how do you know I run a shop?

Nora Well: I walk down Camden Passage, don't I?

David Passing trade.

Nora Not too rough, I hope. And didn't you mention it?

David Did I? Anyway, I've sold my lease. Maybe I did mention it. I want to do pictures next. Like your Paul Sandby. Which I don't see anywhere, by the way.

Nora No.

David takes her in his arms and kisses her. She eagerly responds.

Then he holds her away from him.

David Your Sandby doesn't exist, does it?

Nora No.

This time she kisses him.

David I thought not.

Nora I'm rather more into contemporary.

David	I hate to make this sound formal, but what would you prefer? To carry on here or go upstairs?
Nora	I have watched you before tonight, David.
David	What?
Nora	I don't want to trick you, you see. I hate lies.
David	Lies?
Nora	I clocked this handbill in the delicatessen.
David	Your eyelashes are superb.
Nora	For the Residents' Association.
David	I must return reasonably soon to the Inter-Galactic Space Dock.
Nora	That's it, I thought. And it was. There you were.
David	I was? Where?
Nora	Months ago.
David	Months ago?
Nora	Then you missed a meeting and I'd no chance to move until tonight.
David	You mean you –

Kiss again. Eager.

	You fancied me months ago and I was too stupid to notice?
Nora	I kept out of sight.
David	Incredible.

Again he kisses her. Pulls her into him. She responds then ducks away.

Nora	I'm sorry. I can't compromise.
David	You've changed your mind?

Nora	I must explain.
David	It's not subtle. We either take off our knickers or we don't.
Nora	I want you to be the father of my baby.
David	What?
Nora	You heard.
David	My God.
Nora	I studied you at the meetings.
David	You looked for a father at public meetings?
Nora	I did think about casuals. Pubs and lorry drivers and so on. But none of them were pretty.
David	Wasn't there anyone in your office?
Nora	No. I'm the boss.
David	What sort of an office is it?
Nora	I make TV programmes. Popular stuff. I'm going for the money.
David	Sorry. I'm wandering. It's because I thought I was picking you up.
Nora	You are: after a fashion.
David	Come on. If it was a kosher quickie we'd have done it by now.
Nora	We would.
David	Whereas in our situation we have to set the world to rights first.
Nora	Do you want to go home?
David	Now? Never.

Nora	Why not?
David	I'm in a frenzy of curiosity.
Nora	Super.
David	Why have you told me? Why tell at all?
Nora	For one thing, I don't want to abuse a man in the way in which men have always abused women.
David	A husband-stealer with principles.
Nora	I'm not stealing. I'm a borrower.
David	Why aren't you married? Where's your regular chap?
Nora	I don't have one.
David	Why not?
Nora	You're not disoriented are you?
David	Have you ever had a steady chap?
Nora	Of course. I just never met a man who when we're doing sex treated me as an equal.
David	What?
Nora	You heard. It's a fight. Who's on top? Who's inside which bit of who? Who's calling out for mercy?
David	It isn't a fight.
Nora	It is if we're honest.
David	On no. Oh my God. Philosophies. I'm sorry.
Nora	What d'you want to do? Walk out now or try to prove me wrong?
David	What about love?
Nora	What about it?

David Well. Love. Lifelong. Etcetera.

Nora What you feel for your wife, you mean?

He starts to answer.

Stops.

Starts again.

David I knew you were a handful when I spotted you at the back of the meeting: all demure in expensive scarves.

Nora What I must also say is: if you know of any grounds why you should not become a father, you are on your honour to withdraw.

David Withdraw.

Nora Withdraw.

David In the circumstances, a turn of phrase not glaringly felicitous.

Nora I had my blood test last Friday. I've arranged for you to have yours tomorrow.

David What?

Nora I'll pay, of course. The results come in twenty-four hours, so over Thursday and Friday I'll book into one of those boutique hotels near the Portobello Road.

David The Portobello.

Nora Antiques again. Your cover story.

David I feel like a stud dog.

Nora I don't expect you to show up for an evening performance, of course, but we can do a couple of matinees.

David	What if we draw a blank?
Nora	We keep on until it's bingo.
David	Wouldn't a sperm bank be more efficient?
Nora	I'm a romantic.
David	Oh, dear.
Nora	Aren't you?
David	Who knows, until the vital moment?
Nora	I go for good looks, you see: an ugly child isn't on my list.
David	You don't breed for character?
Nora	You've got what it takes.
David	What's that?
Nora	I trust my judgement.
David	There's one more thing, isn't there?

She is secretly pleased that he realises.

	You want a written contract.
Nora	How did you guess?
David	At Puos Sllebpmac we specialise in Galactic Divinations.
Nora	It's drawn by a very good lawyer.
David	What does it say?
Nora	Shouldn't you read it?
David	Tell me.

Hesitation.

Then she does.

Nora   Once I'm pregnant, we neither meet nor communicate again.

David   Never?

Nora   Never. Agreed?

No answer. She continues.

              The child's mine. You have no rights in it.

David   What if you died?

Nora   My sister will be the guardian.

David   Does she know?

A gesture which seems to say yes.

              So the child would have no rights in me?

Nora   None. It will never know who you are. It will be told that you're wonderful but dead.

David   What about you?

Nora   Me?

David   What rights would you have?

Nora   In you? None.

David   Money?

Nora   I don't need it.

David   My wife?

Nora   I would never communicate with her.

David   Your friends?

Nora   Will never know. It's an accident or a weekend fling. I decided to keep the child.

David   Why?

Nora	They know why.
David	Nevertheless, I would have one responsibility outside the contract.
Nora	No, you wouldn't.
David	I think I would.
Nora	What?
David	The child. I would have to consider the child.
Nora	The child's mine, David. What you get is your actual, irresponsible, impregnating flying fuck.
David	What I must consider, on the child's behalf, is whether or not you would make a good mother.
Nora	What?
David	Can I decide that from a trailer and a couple of matinees?
Nora	How do other people decide?
David	They take time.
Nora	If they love someone they think that's enough.
David	We don't love each other. We're a super-civilised contract job.
Nora	Don't bounce me, David. As to your real question, which is why do I want a child, the answer is that for years and years I didn't but now I do.
David	That's not an answer.
Nora	Oh, David. But it is.
David	No, it isn't.
Nora	Do we have a deal or not?
David	I want to fuck your head off.

Nora	Is it a deal? Will you sign?
David	Yes.
Nora	Wholeheartedly?
David	Wholeheartedly.
Nora	Do you know how you look?
David	How?
Nora	Very smug.
David	Well: it's an adventure: isn't it?

Scene Two   **Nora's House in North London**   **Then**

*A year later. There is a feeling of serenity as **Nora**, singing softly, holds the baby to her to get him to sleep. When she is satisfied, she goes to put him in his cot.*

There is the sound of smashing glass and splintering wood, as the front door is forced open.

***David** bursts in. He is in his top coat and carries a tyre lever.*

David   Nora. Where are you? I know you're here. Where are you?

***Nora** re-appears.*

Where's the baby? Where is he? Where's the baby?

Nora   What are you doing here? What's happened? What's that?

David   I've broken your front lock.

Nora   You've what?

David	Everything snapped. Two weeks ago. I've had you under surveillance.
Nora	Surveillance?
David	Don't gape. What d'you want? Money for a new lock? Is that what's important to you?
Nora	You mean you've spied on me?
David	Sometimes me. Sometimes detectives.
Nora	You're crazy. You must be ill.
David	Didn't you see me?
Nora	What?
David	Watching. Suppose you had done. Would you have spoken?
Nora	Yes. I'd have said: what the hell are you doing?
David	Oh, there's no panic, Nora. I know what I'm doing. He is all right, isn't he?
Nora	All right?
David	The baby.
Nora	What d'you mean?
David	Ten fingers and ten toes and so on.
Nora	Of course he's all right.
David	Wonderful. So it *is* a boy?
Nora	Yes.
David	I knew it. Difficult birth?
Nora	What?
David	Any post-natal depression?
Nora	Never mind me. What about you? You look ill.

David	What gave you that idea?
Nora	David, it's fantastic to see you after so long.
David	As good as a year.
Nora	But it is a bit of a shock and perhaps we should – Suppose we meet somewhere next week, say, so that you can go away now and – Do you see what I mean, David?
David	Not really. Didn't I write you dozens of letters?
Nora	You look awful.
David	What's his name?
Nora	Sam.
David	What does it say on his Birth Certificate?
Nora	It says Sam. It says that he's Sam.
David	Not that.
Nora	What?
David	Who does it say is his father?
Nora	It doesn't.
David	Why not?
Nora	Unknown.
David	Unknown?
Nora	David, you smashed my door in.
David	Unknown?
Nora	We had a contract. You signed it. Our feelings were never life-long, David.
David	Can I see him?
Nora	He's asleep. I must stick to his routine.

David   Sure. I know how that is. Sure. Will you make some tea?

Nora   David tell me what you want.

David   What happened at the birth? Did your mother come down from Manchester?

Nora   Stockport.

David   Stockport. No domestic help?

Nora   A nanny starts next week. Say what you want and go.

He hesitates. Then pulls a paper bag out of his pocket.

What is it?

He gestures. See what's in it.

She does. It contains a book and some chocolates.

She looks at the title of the book.

Shakespeare's Sonnets.

David   The chocs are for you.

Nora   Whose is the book?

David   Sam's.

Nora   He's two weeks old.

David   I've written in it.

She looks.

She is touched but can't believe it.

Do you seriously believe that he won't be curious about me? That he won't want to know?

Nora   Will I fail to describe you?

David   I want a share.

Nora	What?
David	A share.
Nora	Of Sam?
David	And of you.
Nora	No.
David	I'm not a dreamer. I understand. I'll take what I can get. Whatever you decide.
Nora	I've decided to live my own life.
David	There is immense feeling between us.
Nora	No there isn't.
David	There is. You know there is.
Nora	How can you do this to me?
David	It's me who's been abused.
Nora	Abused? Who invented the rules?
David	Nature.
Nora	Men: and then called it nature.
David	He's my son. I've a right to him.
Nora	You haven't. You haven't any right to –
David	Natural law, Nora. That's the law. Natural law.
Nora	What's natural in men is not to care.
David	I'll move in now if you like. With nothing. I'll just stay and never look back.
Nora	David I can't have my happiness at the expense of other people's.
David	So it would make you happy.

Nora   No.

David   You just said it would.

Nora   Why can't you think straight?

David   Why can't you admit that you're mine?

Nora   I'm Sam's mother.

David   Of course you are: you're you: brave, inspiring, mad, magical.

He goes to the drinks and pours one.

Nora   Don't do that. I haven't offered. Leave.

He downs the slug of whisky and pours another.

David   It's no use confining romance to piano bars, Nora. It's got to be in the full light of day.

Nora   David what would your proposals amount to?

David   I haven't made any.

Nora   Moving in now isn't a proposal?

David   Oh. No. Well. Maybe. Why not?

Nora   Why not what?

David   When we first met you'd the confidence to organise anything.

Nora   Your wife, David. Your life. Your children.

David   I've no quarrel with Penny.

Nora   So you don't want to leave her?

David   I want you. Penny could understand that. Why don't you trust me?

Nora   Two households, would that be it? Vying for the master's presence?

David	Not the master.
Nora	The master. The lynch-pin.
David	You'd be the lynch-pin.
Nora	I don't want a life run by a man.
David	It wouldn't be <u>run</u>.
Nora	Yes it would.
David	It would be a compromise like everything else – but still an adventure.
Nora	Defined for all of us by your presence or absence.
David	I'm not at all sure that Penny wouldn't come at it.
Nora	Lots of older women <u>do</u> surrender their dignity.
David	If you knew her you'd not say that.

Silence.

	Something fantastic happened between you and me.
Nora	In the past.
David	So it did happen.
Nora	It's not the point.
David	There is only ever one profound true person in our lives.
Nora	I'm tired, David. If you care for me at all you'll go away.
David	Kiss me.
Nora	No: and actually you stink a bit.
David	Well, I've not been home for three days, have I?
Nora	You're in a hotel?

David   The car.

Nora   To sleep?

David   Yes. But not really.

Nora   Well, you can't have a hot bath here.

David   I want to pick Sam up and hold him.

Nora   No.

David   He's mine.

Nora   David, I don't want to meet you again.

David   I'm going to him.

Nora   No.

David   Stop me.

She tries to stop him but can't.

He shoves her aside.

She rushes at him again and this time he hits her with the tyre-wrench.

She's hurt.

                I'm sorry. I'm very sorry. I'm sorry.

Nora   No you aren't.

David   No. Well. You're wrong and you're a fool. You want to break the rules but it's not allowed.

Nora   Not allowed? Not allowed? Who by?

David   The gods.

Nora   This is a nightmare.

He drains his drink. Pours another.

David   What are you doing?

Nora   I don't know. Why did you hit me?

He drains the drink.

David It's been coming for some time and there must be a decision. I'm outside: in the car: with camera and notebook.

Nora What?

David I'll sit there for an hour. If you come out and bring Sam and sit with me, that's well and good. If you don't so be it: I've got the makings for the cocktail that never fails.

Nora Cocktail?

David A Whisky Mogadon.

She doesn't understand.

Then maybe she does.

> That's it, darling. You come out to me, or I'll kill myself.

And he leaves her.

Scene Three   Nora's Docklands Duplex   Now

Sam *looks round. He hasn't been there for a month. He is twenty and a bit student-scruffy.*

Then his phone rings. He wishes it hadn't, but he answers.

Sam Grandma? No, I haven't had time yet. I only just got here. No. She looks worse than the last time I saw her. Of course I'll get an answer, I'll –

He is about to be interrupted.

> She's coming. I'll call you back. Love you.

Ends the call and pockets the phone.

He tries to seem normal.

Nora *comes in, with mugs and biscuits on a tray.*

Nora	Hot chocolate, Sam. Do you remember? When you were little. Something went wrong, usually me in a fury about work, and you'd say 'Hot chocolate. Make it better.'
Sam:	Amazeballs.
Nora	Oh dear. Sorry. Did I embarrass you yet again?
Sam	The thing is, Mum, I don't actually remember.
Nora	You must remember.
Sam	You always say that, but I don't. Kids don't.
Nora	You've not deliberately wiped it, have you?
Sam	Things that are more interesting intervene. Do you know what I mean?
Nora	I must do, I suppose. Of course I must. Mustn't I? It's still a bit galling, though, to be a mother, and look back at events, and be the only one who remembers them.
Sam	It's life, Mum. Time's inevitable obliteration of everything.

He drinks.

It's very good.

	Wow.
Nora	It's a new recipe. Chocolate, cream, powdered malt, and a bay leaf.
Sam	It's mega. Do bay trees grow here in Docklands?

Scene Three

Nora Some do.

Sam Where?

Nora In the atria of banks.

Sam In tubs.

Nora Yes.

Sam I hate banks.

Nora Then you won't be allowed in to pick the leaves, will you?

Sam Dunno. There might be an anti-capitalist sit-in.

Nora I thought you gave up on anti-capitalism.

Sam I put it on hold until after the exams.

Takes a biscuit.

Doesn't want it.

Puts it back.

Nora What's the matter?

Sam What? Nothing.

Nora Who was that on the phone?

Sam Why do you think you need to know?

Nora You mean it was that girl.

Sam No, actually.

Nora Your grandmother.

It was. Yes.

Why can't she just sit in the care home and shut up?

Sam Would you?

Nora   What?

Sam   Sorry. But would you?

Nora   She could have moved down here. I even said I'd buy her a flat in this building. But no, no, she – It's her life, isn't it? Her life's up North and mine's down here.

Sam   It is, and she worries about you, like the way you worry about me.

They both consider this, and where it leaves them.

Then they both speak at once.

       She knows that you saw the specialist a week ago and she's worried because –

Nora   I had decisions to make before I phoned either of you but –

They both stop.

Sam   I did explain. I said that since the operation two years ago you have these routine check-ups, and that if there's any change we'll be told. Unfortunately Grandma thinks you fob her off, so she asks me, day after day. So when I didn't hear from you either I –

A gesture finishes it.

Nora   You decided to appear, and here you are.

Sam   Yes.

Nora   It's terminal.

Sam   What?

Nora   Terminal.

Sam   It can't be.

Nora   It is.

Sam   Come on. There must be some—

Nora   There isn't.

Sam tries to speak but can't.

Sorry.

Sam   Why didn't you tell us? What's wrong with us?

Nora   Nothing's wrong with you.

Sam   In your eyes there must be.

Nora   In my eyes I had a bigger decision.

Sam   I can put off my exams, you know. I can talk to the College. They'll understand. I can live here and be with you and –

Stops. Too many thoughts.

Nora   Won't it soon be the long vacation anyway?

Sam   What?

Nora   Aren't you going to Italy with that girl?

Sam   Italy?

Then he remembers.

Yes, but –

But he still can't find what to say.

Nora   Are either of us grown-up enough for this?

Sam   Dunno. Aren't you?

Nora   You do remember saying 'Hot chocolate', don't you?

Sam   Yes.

Of course he remembers.

          How long?

Nora   Have I got?

Yes, says his gesture.

          Months. Some. Maybe.

Sam   Maybe?

Nora   Maybe.

Sam *finds it hard to compute this.*

Sam   Why are you so calm?

Nora   Am I?

Sam   Are you in pain?

Nora   Not especially.

Sam   Especially?

Nora   Tired. Headaches. Unable to do things.

Sam   But surely they can – Did you ask them? What –? Can't they?

Nora   They offered. Chemo. Radiation. Hair falling out. Dizzy. Having to wear nappies. Wanting to vomit but can't. Who needs it again? I said no.

Sam   No?

Nora   No. So I need to ask you a favour.

Sam   A favour?

Nora   Come with me.

Sam   You want me to go somewhere?

Nora   Paris.

Sam	Paris? When? Why?
Nora	Two nights, maybe. Then the TGV. Zurich. The Baur au Lac.
Sam	Zurich?
Nora	Dinner at the Kronenhalle, even. If I can. Why not?
Sam	Are you crazy?
Nora	Not about the clinic, no.
Sam	Clinic.
Nora	The one where I can end life on my terms.
Sam	Jesus.
Nora	You can't face it?
Sam	Grandma said it: you'll be a control freak to the very last gasp.
Nora	I should swat the pair of you.
Sam	You're dying, mother. Do you even have the strength to swat a bluebottle?
Nora	Buzz buzz.
Sam	Don't flirt.
Nora	Say you'll come with me.
Sam	You've already arranged it, haven't you? Haven't you?

Silence.

But yes.

Was that the decision you had to make?

Nora No, that was easy. The decision was to tell you about your father.

Sam You have told me.

Nora No.

Sam One night stand. Pregnant. Before anything could happen he died.

Nora No.

Sam No?

Nora No.

Sam So what? He's still alive? What?

Nora This is hard, Sam. I don't want you to hate me.

Sam Why would I hate you? You've not told me lies, have you? Why?

Nora Just listen. It was when the business had taken off. Contracts for drama.

Sam Soap opera.

Nora Lots of episodes.

Sam Money ripped out of the budgets.

Nora Don't start that. It's what brought you everything.

Sam Sorry.

Nora What will you do? Give it back?

Sam I said sorry.

Awkward silence.

But she must go on.

Nora I'd reached a point in life. I wanted a child but I didn't need a man. So I picked him.

Sam	Him?
Nora	Your father.
Sam	You mean –

He realises what she is saying.

	Oh.
Nora	Yes.
Sam	How could you do that?
Nora	Very easily.
Sam	You didn't think about later?
Nora	Later? What was later? Have you missed a father?
Sam	Wasn't given the chance, was I? Sent to boarding-school. Alma pater.

She does not want to address this.

No. I haven't missed a father. Have I? I don't know.

She starts to speak. Stops.

Is that the point? He's not dead at all? Is that the point?

Nora	No.
Sam	He is dead.
Nora	Yes.
Sam	When? Recently? What are you –?
Nora	Stop it.
Sam	Stop? First you tell me you're dying and then will I go with you to some suicide clinic and then –
Nora	Just listen. We had an agreement. He'd get me pregnant and then never see me again.

Sam If you never saw him again how do you know what happened to him?

Nora He couldn't keep his side of the bargain.

Sam You mean he wanted you? He loved you? He wanted me? He – Did you love him?

Nora That wasn't it. Don't interrupt. I don't want to remember it. He was wonderful. I thought so. I did think so. But he lost himself. His whole life was a falsehood, of course. He said that if I didn't – He'd kill himself if I didn't -

Sam Didn't what?

Nora I don't want to remember.

Sam If you didn't what?

Nora I'm sorry, Sam, I'm sorry, I –

She is too full of emotion and manages to run out.

Sam Mother? If you didn't what? Mother?

He goes after her.

Scene Four   Nora's North London House   Then

Nora holds baby Sam in her arms.

David is still in his car in the street outside.

Nora knows that to save everything she believes in she must stand fast.

Nora What's happening, Sam? Oh, Sam, what is this? It's Sam and Mummy keeping very calm because – Ssh – It's sleepytime. Goosey goosey Gander, where do you wander? Daddy may be sitting in his car with a bottle of whisky but we can't go out there, Sam, because it's Sam's sleepytime, and for Mummy to cling to everything she believes in she must be firm. She mustn't go out. We have peeked, though, haven't we, and he saw us didn't he, although he pretended not to. Silly Daddy. He's been out there for two and a half hours and it's getting dark. But Mummy can't go out. If she goes out she'll throw away all her respect for herself, and any chance of real respect from Daddy. He'd think that whenever he whistled she'd come. Of course I do want to. I do. I mean, I'm angry but I want to help him. I want to say: it's all right. It's all right. We love you, and life's never as bad as it seems, and when we're generous to people it's wonderful. But if Mummy goes out and tries to say that, do you know what, Sam? He'll throw my feelings in my face. He won't respect them. He'll crash and bash like he did earlier: smashing our door in because he thinks it's his right, and that his feelings are some law of the gods. Daddy's too angry, Sam, and he's very hurt, because I've said boo to his law of the gods. We have to give him time, Sam. Sorry, darling. Ssh. Don't grizzle. Ssh. Of course you won't be as silly as he is. You'll be tall and strong and upright, as a man should be, but you won't – Mummy can explain all this again when you're – Well, when you're a young man, and we don't have secrets. I'll make money. I'll work hard and make money, and when we've lots of money we won't be hurt for our principles. We might even be friends with Daddy and, who knows, things might happen so that he can live with us and – We mustn't dream that, Sam. We mustn't.

What we must do is live on our own terms. We can't be blackmailed. Should I take another peep? If it's too dark he won't see us. But we won't see him either, will we, so we'll stay and put Sam in his cot. Then we'll phone for a locksmith. One of those emergency people in the Yellow Pages. Daddy can watch them repair our door and – Actually, when it's dark he'll drive off, won't he? He has to. How can he come back after his stupid threats and bluster? Drunks do, of course, but he's not a proper drunk, is he? He's just pride and worked-up ego and he won't listen. What I should say is how dare he? How dare he provoke me and make me lash out? He thinks that because I'm a Mummy he can shame me until I hate myself. Then I'll feel guilty and do what he wants. I won't hurt him because to hurt him hurts me more. And it does. But in the long run, Sam, what's the worst? The compromise is the worst, like my mummy, I mean your Grandma, pretending all the time to be whatever it is that won't upset my father. I mean, Grandpa. But he is upset. Every day he's angry with her and that's the worst, Sam. It destroys our joy in life, and it's why we can't go out to the car, my darling. Your Daddy needs time, Sam, to find the answer in himself.

Scene Five   **Nora's Docklands Duplex**   **Now**

Later. **Sam** *comes back in. The room is the same but he's a bit different, he realises.*

Then **Nora**. *Drained but more free, perhaps.*

Nora	Sorry. I'm sorry I cried so much. Hard to go through it again. Sorry.
Sam	Hot chocolate.
Nora	Hot chocolate.
Sam	When did you realise what he'd done?
Nora	Well you went off to sleep, didn't you, and so I put you in your cot which was next to my bed and because I was exhausted I lay down myself and woke up in my clothes because there were lights and emergency vehicles. Some passer-by called 999. There's a man in a parked car and I think he's dead.
Sam	Nobody came to the door.
Nora	No. And it was all in his head, you see, the detectives and surveillance and – all a fantasy. Then as soon as it was light I drove up North.
Sam	To Grandma.
Nora	Grandma. A week later, was it – No, it can't have been. Three weeks. Four. His wife appeared. Jolly lucky to catch me. I only came back to put the house on the market.
Sam	But you were upset.
Nora	Still shaking.
Sam	Did you blame yourself?

Nora   Sometimes.

Sam   Yes.

Nora   Will you?

Sam   Maybe.

Nora   Yes.

Sam   Did his wife?

Nora   No.

Sam   Why not?

Nora   She knew everything. My whole scheme and everything.

Sam   How?

Nora   David told her.

Sam   Why?

Nora   I think that they were the permissives and I was the naïve one.

Sam   I don't understand.

Nora   At the time I thought "presumptuous bitch" but actually she was fantastic. Posh. Her own money. A consultant surgeon. Older than him. He was the night porter in some hell-hole near Victoria Station.

Sam   You've always said he was an antiques dealer.

Nora   He met her as a patient in her NHS clinic. Great looks. Great chatter. So she fucked him and married him, as who wouldn't have done, in a way, and put him in bespoke shirts and set him up as a dealer. And so on and so forth.

Scene Five 35

Sam Why did she come to see you?

Nora She wanted to know what happened. Had he come inside or just sat in the car? When I told her she said quite correct. Don't reproach yourself. It's hard but what she'd done was the past, she said, and what I did was the future.

Sam The future?

Nora Yes.

Sam What of?

Nora Men and women.

Sam Oh.

Nora He couldn't live with that, she said, and I said that I should have made him understand that he could change but still be a man, as it were.

Sam As it were?

Nora He could still be dominant when he fucked us.

Sam Oh.

Nora I mean it's not the men we're vile over so much, is it? It's the children.

Sam does not know what to say.

Oh, come on. I've not shocked you, have I?

Sam Medea.

Nora What?

Sam Greek tragedy.

Nora What are you talking about? You mean my cancer's some sort of punishment?

Sam No. I mean I had a spat about Medea with my superior.

Nora Has your headache gone?

Sam What?

Nora Sorry. I mean: has my headache gone?

Sam I don't know. Has it?

Nora I need my painkiller.

Sam Now?

Nora Where's my handbag?

He finds it.

She rummages in it.

Finds what she wants.

A screw-top bottle.

Sam So Grandma knew everything that happened. And Auntie Mary.

Nora drinks.

Nora Thank you waiter. Almost as good as the Brunello. Yes. Mary knew. Took it with her to the grave.

Sam What is that?

Nora An opium derivative. Absolute bliss.

Sam They prescribed it?

Nora Pain control.

Sam Why have you told me about David?

Nora I'm dying.

Sam I can't absolve you.

Nora	I don't think I've sinned.
Sam	But I do have a question about my own pain.
Nora	You're in pieces?
Sam	Afraid so. Medea.
Nora	What about her?
Sam	It's fine to be mad at her husband, I said in my essay, but killing the kids seems a bit hard. I mean, what have they done, actually? Well. They're like me, of course. They've been born. My supervisor said don't be flippant, she said. Consider the deeper issues.
Nora	Did she say what they were?
Sam	No, and until a few minutes ago I'd no idea but now I remember how I was when that girl dumped me and Medea and David in the car and – what's wrong?
Nora	You made it up with that girl.
Sam	Yes. But when she dumped me I – Well I think David sat in the car and he had this notion that when you discovered that he was dead you'd be there, somehow, and he'd look at you and say you see? I told you so, you stupid bitches.
Nora	That's a deeper issue?
Sam	I'm a man. Like him. Are my instincts wrong as well?
Nora	You're not a man.
Sam	I'm not?
Nora	Not to me. You're my child. Always.

Sam Ye Gods. Medea.

Nora I need a hot water bottle.

She drinks more painkiller.

Sam As you know, darling, I've had two friends who overdosed. One insisted that he was the Inca of Peru and the next day he was found dead in a phone box.

Nora What?

Sam Shouldn't you measure your dosage?

Nora Yes. But what does it matter?

Sam Are you fit to be on your own? No. You're not.

Nora Full time. Starting tomorrow.

Sam Carers?

Nora I think you knew about me anyway, because you quizzed the specialist. Didn't you?

Sam You've arranged for carers?

Nora I have. Did you know?

Sam More or less.

So there we are.

What else haven't you told me?

Nora I've lost sight in this eye again. It's the tumour. Last time it took two days to come back.

Sam What else?

Nora You'll need people. You know. Like family.

Sam If I had any.

Nora You do.

Sam	What?
Nora	Siblings. David's kids. Two brothers and a sister.
Sam	A sister?
Nora	Half-sister. I wanted a girl. I so wanted a girl as well as you but after what happened I couldn't trust anyone. Or myself. My judgement of men. Made money instead. No consolation.
Sam	You mustn't reproach yourself.
Nora	No. Isn't awful it but?
Sam	You mean: but isn't it awful?
Nora	Do I?
Sam	Yes.
Nora	Is it?
Sam	Not as awful as seeing you ill.
Nora	I think I should lie down, actually. D'you mind?

She gets up.

Holds out her hand for his support.

He gives it.

Sam	How old's my sister?
Nora	Half-sister.
Sam	Half-sister.
Nora	At least thirty. Why?
Sam	Watch how you walk.

Slowly, they go out to her bedroom.

40 Sam's Father

Scene Six   Nora's Docklands Duplex   Now

At least a month later. **Sam** *and* **Nora** *are dressed to travel. She has elbow crutches.*

Silence. Waiting to be told that it is time to go down to the car.

Nora *starts to ask a question but stops.*

Sam   It's okay, Mum. Under control. They'll buzz me when it's time.

There's still a residue of worry.

There'll be wheelchairs everywhere. You'll be whizzed through Security and onto the plane.

Nora   Your cuff's held together by a safety-pin.

Sam   Yes.

Should she ask why?

She manages not to.

Sam   Are you okay?

Nora   I'm disappointed.

Sam   What?

Nora   After I'm dead I won't know what happens, will I?

Sam   This Switzerland jaunt was your call, you know.

Nora   It just came sooner than expected. I know. Anyway. Sorry we missed out on Paris.

Sam   It's okay.

Nora   Perhaps you and that girl can go. To the restaurant. And remember me.

Sam   The restaurant.

Nora   Lucas-Carton.

Sam   The one with the Art Nouveau interior.

Nora   Yes.

Sam   I used to hate Art Nouveau.

They think about it.

                   Will having the money stop me from being normal?

Nora   What? What's normal? I don't know. What are you talking about?

Sam   Money from your dumbed-down television.

Nora   Maybe it was the audience that changed. Lost interest. Weren't as educated. Whatever. Ever think about that?

Sam   I'm beginning to.

Nora   Does it depress you?

Sam   Yes.

Nora   I suppose it might be why I sold the company.

Sam   And to cash in.

Nora   Yes.

Silence.

Then she points, as a preliminary to asking again about the shirt cuff.

But he heads her off.

Sam   Moment of passion. Clothes ripped off. Button a casualty. That girl.

Nora   Wonderful.

Sam	Then we argued.
Nora	What about?
Sam	Can't remember.
Nora	Oh.
Sam	Then she walked out.
Nora	Again? Why? I know why. You're infuriating.
Sam	But she texted me.
Nora	What I wanted to ask was: don't you have another clean shirt?
Sam	Not of this colour.
Nora	You'll set off the security alarms.

He manages not to rise to this.

And none of it is what really agitates her.

	I never felt guilt over David, you know. I felt rage, and guilt because I didn't feel guilty.
Sam	Did I hear that? I don't think I did.
Nora	Sorry. I spent years making sure I never admitted it. My air cushion will be in the car, won't it?
Sam	Don't worry.

She wants to say "I'm not" but hasn't the energy.

Then:

	Anyway. National Gallery, she texted. Meet me outside.
Nora	No surprise. She does talk very well about painting.
Sam	What?
Nora	She visited me.

Sam   She what? When?

Nora   Just go on.

He wants to ask more.

   Week last. Last week. Go on.

Sam   All right. We met and the first thing she did was slap me across the face, which excited the curiosity of the passing tourists. Stop being tragic, she said, which I suppose I was being. Go back, she said.

Nora   Go back?

Sam   To my sister.

Nora   Sister?

Sam   Half-sister.

Nora   Oh.

Sam   Winifred. So I phoned. On answer. Left a message. Apologising. No reply. Texted. Again no reply.

Nora   When was this?

Sam   Monday.

Nora   You mean this shirt's been washed and ironed and put away unmended and –

Sam   Stop it. I'm sorry.

Nora   So you should be.

And they both know why.

After a moment she voices it.

   A month ago you told me that you couldn't find Winifred.

Sam   Yes.

Nora	But you did.
Sam	Yes.
Nora	You saw her?
Sam	Yes.
Nora	My God. Where?
Sam	Cheltenham.
Nora	Cheltenham?
Sam	It's where she lives. She hung up when I said who I was but her husband persuaded her, it seems, and eventually she called back and – When I went he wasn't there, unfortunately. Sacked by the bank. Another new job interview.
Nora	You and Winifred quarrelled?
Sam	They've got two kids and she works part-time in a flower shop. One of the brothers is in Canada and the other has problems. His father's death was his fault, he thinks.

***Nora** starts to speak but stops.*

> They knew about the suicide. Had to. All over the local papers and an inquest.

***Nora** has an unvoiced question.*

> You? No. They didn't know about you. Their mother never mentioned you until years later. One of many affairs, she said. David could never decide what he wanted. True?

Nora	Maybe.
Sam	Maybe. And they didn't know at all about me and – well, it was a very sunny day and we went into

the back garden, which was a mess, really, what with the dogs and the children, and I'd not been there long but it seemed okay until she said that her next-door neighbours had gone to Corfu for a month, whereas she hadn't had an actual break for three years, and why had nobody told her that I existed and life went to pieces after her father died and her mother had drunk herself to death, actually, said the people in the care home, and it was your fault and my fault and why did my going to see her do anything except make everything worse and I was dumb because I realised –

Stops.

Nora What?

Sam Winifred had no idea that her mother had visited you.

Nora No.

Sam So there was another way of dealing with it all. Another story. Another David. Another Nora. Another –

He stops for a moment.

She waits.

I think I said something about not choosing our parents. Something naff, anyway, and she sort of chased me out and we knocked things over and then there was the postman.

Nora The postman?

Sam Well she was pushing me and hitting me in the chest and then she slammed the door on me, and like a complete arse I shouted through the letter-box. "The sexual revolution was an aerial bombardment," I shouted, "and we're in the wreckage and I'm more or less okay but you're not so—". At which moment the postman arrived. The shorts. The bag over the shoulder. The lot. And he said "Excuse me, mate," and put a postcard of Corfu and six dog biscuits through the door.

Nora Dog biscuits.

Sam "Keeps the buggers onside," he said.

Nora Of course.

Sam I was on my hands and knees and felt completely ridiculous, so I got up and slunk back to the train.

Nora Weeks ago.

Sam Yes.

Nora God. Weeks in which I didn't die.

Sam No.

Nora And you're telling me all this now because you've suddenly heard back from her.

Sam This morning. When the carers were helping you to shower.

Nora You spoke?

Sam She texted.

Nora To say what?

Sam Try again. Please. On neutral ground.

Nora Neutral.

Sam She suggested Swindon railway station.

Nora Swindon.

Sam	Yes.
Nora	Glamorous.
Sam	Don't be snide.
Nora	Snide?
Sam	You're a provincial snobby-boots.
Nora	Never.
Sam	Look outside. We're on the eighteenth glitzed-up floor, for God's sake.
Nora	Property's an investment. Have you heard from your grandmother?
Sam	What? Yes. She's okay. But I promised you'd phone.
Nora	I'd have asked her to join us but she'd just have behaved as though it was her committing assisted suicide not me.

Sam *decides to ignore this.*

	You will keep paying her bills, won't you?
Sam	You've set it up already and of course I'll – And she's ok, Mum. Up North and safe.
Nora	Will you sell this flat?
Sam	I don't want to think what I'll do.

Silence.

Nora	Did you text back?
Sam	To Winifred? No.
Nora	Why not?
Sam	I'm too nervous.

Nora Do it now. You'll be thrilled. Swindon. End of next week.

Sam Right.

He punches the keys.

Nora God knows if there'll be a refreshment room.

Sam Which was guaranteed in Grandma's day.

Nora It was.

Silence.

Send it.

Sam *presses the send button.*

Done.

Sam Satisfied?

Nora And I may as well confess. I've got my own surprise news.

Sam What?

Nora That girl. She's coming with us. She'll meet us at Heathrow.

Sam You mean you -

Nora Yes. I did. What's happening? Why isn't it time?

A placatory gesture.

She relaxes.

But she has a question.

Nora Do you think that this is how your father felt?

Sam What?

Nora In the car. Waiting to die. After he'd shovelled down the pills.

He looks. A bit shaken, actually.

Sam	Mum, whatever thoughts he had, they were whisky thoughts.
Nora	And whisky waiting.
Sam	Yes.
Nora	Aren't you a bit young to know about that?
Sam	In today's world? No.

They think about it.

Nora	But he did love me.
Sam	Hot chocolate.

They think about this, too.

Nora Anyway, to answer what you wanted to ask but didn't. I asked that girl and she said that she agreed with me. You can't come back from Zurich on your own, can you?

If he wants to say something he can't quite think what it would be.

So they wait.

Then his phone bleeps.

He reads the message.

Sam Okay. It's the driver. We can go.

Slowly, she gets herself up and they make their way to the door.

Then his phone beeps again and they stop.

Nora Oh no. Not a hold up.

***Sam** checks it.*

Sam It's Winifred. She's confirmed.

Nora It'll be difficult for you, but very good. And we're off on our travels, aren't we?

They slowly move again.

The End of the Play

Hannah Vine

CHARACTERS

Delamere   a retired professor

Barbara   a pulp biographer

Clementine   an assistant in a charity shop

The scene is Delamere's study in his house in Cambridge, in the present day.

Scene One   Delamere's Study   Afternoon

***Barbara** is a pulp biographer. As she waits she takes in the room. She is alerted by a photograph. She picks it up and scrutinises it. She puts it down just in time as **Delamere** arrives with a tea tray. He is a retired academic.*

Barbara You shouldn't have gone to so much trouble.

Delamere Well: all one has to do is boil water.

Barbara I mean, it's very generous of you to see me.

Not at all, says his smile and gesture.

Did you check me out on the internet?

Delamere The internet? You mean one can - ? Of course. The internet. But I'm sure that you did your research on me.

Barbara Did you bother to read any of my other books?

Delamere No. Sorry. That is to say, modern life having passed me by, I did a bookshop rummage.

Barbara That sounds like fun. What is it?

Delamere One stands there, and flicks over a page or two. Milk?

Barbara No.

Delamere Sugar?

Barbara No.

Delamere Neither. What about your driver?

Barbara He has his flask of coffee, and a book of Monster Sudoku.

Delamere Very professional.

Barbara He's not a luxury, I'm afraid. I'm still disqualified.

Delamere From driving?

Barbara Driving.

Delamere Why?

Barbara Speed.

Delamere Marvellous.

Barbara It raises me in your estimation?

Delamere Well, speed is a sort of club, isn't it? Or used to be.

Barbara Whereas what I write is mere sensationalism.

Delamere I did read in a newspaper that your advance for this book was half a million. Is that true?

Barbara More or less.

Delamere My word. You must be sensational.

Barbara It's not me, Professor. It's who I write about.

Delamere Still: publishers must believe in you.

Barbara I've made them money, if that's what you mean.

Delamere Was it your own idea to write about Hannah Vine?

Barbara Not at all. She was suggested by a friend.

Delamere Really?

Barbara I'm not caught up by feminism. I mean, I know it's true. But I'm afraid I'm a get ahead in the world as it is sort of girl.

Delamere But you've read Hannah's books?

Barbara Before? No. Not especially.

Delamere Not especially.

Barbara I was aware of them, if you know what I mean.

Delamere I do. Whereas your friend was a reader?

Barbara She was a skimmer, but intrigued by what happened to Hannah. It was right up my street, she said.

Delamere Easy Street? Queer Street? What street?

Barbara Vulgar Curiosity Street. It made me think "Wow!" So I approached publishers and did a deal.

Delamere Is that my cue to think "Wow"?

Barbara Sorry. Can't help noticing. That's a charming photograph.

Delamere It was their wedding day.

Barbara He's an army officer.

Delamere Yes.

Barbara My own son's getting married next month.

Delamere Congratulations.

Barbara You must wonder, I suppose, how I have a son when my publicity proclaims that I'm gay.

Delamere What I did read about you was for a book jacket very measured.

Barbara Wolverhampton. Much older sister. Mum and Dad ran a fish and chip shop.

Delamere But you, said the blurb, found your way to London.

Barbara On the coach.

Delamere And talked yourself into a job on what had been your favourite teenage magazine.

Barbara What it left out was that I'd said "Sod salt and vinegar!" and gone bonkers.

Delamere Bonkers?

Barbara Drugs.

Delamere Hard?

Barbara Sniffs.

Delamere Sniffs?

Barbara Glue bags. Brain zips. Whoopee!

Delamere Glue must be sticky, surely.

Barbara Then the syringe. Jesus on the mainline.

Delamere Mainline?

Barbara Tell him what you need.

Delamere What did you?

Barbara Mercy.

Delamere What did you get?

Barbara Excluded from school. Shoplifting. Juvenile Court. Social Services. Was I a lesbian or not? That was the point. I couldn't decide. So I fucked the Probation Officer.

Delamere A man?

Barbara Yes.

Delamere He was the father?

Barbara Yes.

Delamere Married?

Barbara More or less.

Delamere   Scandal?

Barbara   No. I never gave him away, did I?

Delamere   Very civil of you.

Barbara   Well, he was more adrift than me, really. He'd failed as an actor.

Delamere   Oh dear.

Barbara   He did sort of start me on biographies, though.

Delamere   At the time?

Barbara   Later. When I thought about it. Real life was punchier than what I could make up.

Delamere   Did you take your son with you to London?

Barbara   School holidays. Mum had him most of the time.

Delamere   Where is he now?

Barbara   California. Silicon Valley.

Delamere   Which leaves you alone?

Barbara   Not always. But I do seem to give most girls the shove.

Delamere   Do they never shove you?

Barbara   It has been known.

Delamere   Why are you telling me all this?

Barbara   You have to, when you do what I do.

Delamere   Which is what, would you say?

Barbara   Muck rake.

Delamere   So-called exposé biographies.

Barbara   One can't have hidden muck of one's own. I always re-hash mine at Book Fairs.

Delamere But the people you write about do have secrets.

Barbara Yes. Or they invent them.

Delamere They invent muck?

Barbara For publicity.

Delamere What a world. And these are living people?

Barbara Yes.

Delamere Hannah Vine's dead.

No reply.

What muck did she have, do you reckon?

Barbara Why did you agree to see me?

Delamere Why wouldn't I?

Barbara Until now you've refused all requests to discuss her.

Delamere Yes. Well. I suppose that in my old age I believe that someone has to tell a bit of the truth.

Barbara Only a bit?

Delamere I only know a bit.

Barbara Yet she wrote very warmly of your influence.

Delamere She did.

Barbara Were you aware of that influence at the time?

Delamere No. Not really.

Barbara Why not?

Delamere She was a student. One among many.

Barbara What about later?

Delamere Later?

Barbara When she wrote that she'd have to reject what you stood for?

Delamere Well. Later was later.

Barbara And you no longer knew her.

He does not answer.

Do you mind if I record you?

Delamere You should. I'd prefer it. Can you send me a transcript?

Barbara Of course.

Delamere For approval?

Barbara Of your own words? Yes.

Delamere Thank you.

Barbara Not of my gloss on them.

Delamere Oh.

Her little digital recorder is ready.

Barbara Are we recording on these terms or not?

Delamere What will you ask me?

Barbara Hannah as a student. Her personality. The gist of her writings. The TV interview and subsequent shit-storm. Her death.

He gestures: go ahead. I agree.

She presses the button.

Interview with Professor Delamere. Cambridge. October 27. Testing.

Machine Interview with Professor Delamere. Cambridge. October 27. Testing.

Stops it.

Barbara Ready?

Delamere Ready.

She starts the machine and off they go.

Barbara Professor Delamere. How did you meet Hannah Vine?

Delamere She was a freshman. At that time her own college had no Director of Studies in English, so they sent her to me.

Barbara That's English Literature?

Delamere Yes.

Barbara And you supervised her for how many terms?

Delamere Three?

Barbara Her entire first year.

Delamere Until her own college made an appointment.

Barbara And that was Doctor Morris.

Delamere Yes.

Barbara Whom you knew?

Delamere Not well. She was American, on a Visiting Fellowship.

Barbara By many accounts, it was she who opened Hannah's eyes to feminism.

Delamere So they say.

Barbara You don't agree?

Delamere Have you talked to her?

Barbara Yes.

Delamere What did she say?

Barbara She thinks she helped, but that Hannah would have got there anyway.

Delamere I'm sure that's true.

Barbara But it was you, she said, who first set Hannah's mind in motion.

Delamere Maybe. But it is hard to know. First years are very early stages.

Barbara Do you think you gave her specific ideas?

Delamere No. I just talked about writing.

Barbara What does that mean?

Delamere Well: what seems good. What may be meretricious. What did the writer seek to do and how was it achieved or not. At Hannah's age people haven't read very much.

Barbara How old was she?

Delamere Eighteen?

Barbara Mature for that age, or not?

Delamere Probably not.

Barbara That's how she struck you?

Delamere How can I explain this? She struck me in retrospect.

Barbara When she was published and became famous, you mean?

Delamere Yes. It prompted me to try to remember. What had I noticed at the time?

Barbara What had you?

Delamere Not much.

She waits.

I mean, what distorts memory is later information.

Barbara You knew that she'd won a scholarship?

Delamere Yes; and that she was working-class and from the provinces was obvious, I suppose, but…

But it was all he needed to know, really.

Barbara Father a bus driver, mother a cleaner, home a council tower block…

Delamere Why would she have told me that? We were reading the metaphysical poets.

Barbara Was she pleased with herself?

Delamere What?

Barbara Pleased with herself.

Delamere As a person?

Barbara For being at Cambridge.

Delamere I've no idea.

Barbara But it's an elite, isn't it?

Delamere She was still a schoolgirl, more or less. Seeking her depth.

Barbara What sort of questions did she ask?

Delamere What?

Barbara Questions.

Delamere Oh. I don't recall. Yes, I do. Of course I do. She once said: what *is* sentimentality?

Barbara What is it?

Delamere Didn't Leavis define it as emotion in excess of the facts?

Barbara Who's Leavis?

Delamere A dead critic.

Barbara But the point is that Hannah's intelligence did show itself?

Delamere It did.

Barbara But you were never aware of the warrior element?

Delamere Students are students, you know. Not many go on to be warriors.

Barbara Were you surprised when Hannah did?

Delamere Yes. No. I'm not sure. Maybe. I mean, the cleverest man I taught drank himself to death five years later. Who knows about people?

Barbara So to sum up this first introductory chapter, as it were. How at the time did you think that you'd helped Hannah?

Delamere One tries to welcome people into the life of the mind. Is that pompous?

Barbara Probably. But it'll do. Did you find Hannah Vine attractive?

Delamere What?

Barbara Attractive.

Delamere As a personality?

Barbara Sexually.

Delamere She was my student.

Barbara You mean you never once gave her the eye-over?

Delamere Have I looked at you in that way?

Barbara Briefly.

Delamere And then what?

Barbara Put it aside.

Delamere Maybe that's your answer.

Barbara Did Hannah look at you?

Delamere She listened. I would say intently.

Barbara Could she have pulled you if she'd wanted to?

Delamere She was my student.

Barbara Come on, Professor. Could she pull?

Delamere Miss Barbara, we're not –

Barbara Call me Babs.

Delamere Babs. Indeed. Well, Babs - Miss Babs - we're not speaking of today. We're speaking of a different epoch.

Barbara Tell me about it.

Delamere Your publisher may well want something sexed-up and sensational. But our lives weren't like that.

Barbara What were they like?

Delamere Because there was respect there was constraint.

Barbara No bum pinchers?

Delamere What?

Barbara No nipple flickers? Office gropers? Gross assumptions of superiority.

Delamere Stop your machine.

She stops it. Waits.

        Are you interviewing me or making a speech?

Barbara   Background analysis.

Delamere   Did Hannah Vine ever write about bottom pinchers?

Barbara   She did describe an encounter with a flasher.

This he had more or less forgotten.

Delamere   True. I apologise.

Barbara   Thank you.

Delamere   Didn't she also say somewhere that older women had been vile to her because she was thin?

Barbara   As a thin woman myself I won't raise that.

Delamere   Understood. I won't be provocative.

Barbara   May I re-start?

Go ahead.

She re-starts.

        But women's lives, Professor. Weren't they about men? Wasn't that the problem?

Delamere   Man's love is of his life a thing apart. 'Tis woman's whole existence.

Barbara   Did somebody write that?

Delamere   Lord Byron.

Barbara   A dodgy numero if ever there was one.

Delamere   Dodginess and perception are not of necessity mutually exclusive. As for our lives –

Barbara   Hannah Vine's life.

Delamere Hannah Vine famous, Miss Babs, was not Hannah Vine my student. Hannah Vine famous was tall and elegant and there was space around her. My student was inconspicuous and wore mousey cardigans. I did not want to be pulled, as you put it, and women then were treated with a great deal more respect than they are today.

Barbara Nonsense.

Delamere It's not nonsense.

Barbara Feminism has led to less respect?

Delamere Of course. And the evidence is everywhere around you.

Barbara You mean that women should never have striven for – You old shocker, you!

Delamere This is it, you see. What Hannah Vine predicted. Political correctness has so constricted the rules of debate that it's almost impossible to discuss anything.

Barbara Was that her vital contribution?

Delamere More like her sorrow, wouldn't you say?

Barbara Can I ask you what it was you taught her that she rejected?

He gathers himself.

Delamere What she actually wrote was that she wanted everything I'd said to be true, but couldn't persuade herself that it was.

Barbara What had you said?

Delamere It wasn't me so much as what I, and others, seemed to represent. What I'd known and experienced. Which is to say, the last high days of the English Faculty.

Barbara What does that mean, exactly?

Delamere Well. Think of where we were in the world.

Barbara Where were we?

Delamere In much the same place as today, except that today is rather worse.

Barbara Oh.

Delamere You realise that in the Nineteenth Century science destroyed much of the literal truth of religion, and with it the grand narrative of mankind, the meaning of life and the basis of right and wrong and moral action?

Barbara Er – I just thought that school prayers were a drag.

Delamere You never have hours of desolation?

Barbara Got me. I do.

Delamere How do you fill them?

Barbara I tell myself I'm important, even when I know it's bullshit.

Delamere Precisely.

Barbara So go on.

Delamere What could replace religion? What would be the grand narrative of existence? Material progress, it seemed. The visions of that last of the Old Testament prophets Karl Marx. Being on the right side of history. That's what would be true and moral.

Barbara   Politics…

Delamere Economics…

Barbara   But it didn't end up that way.

Delamere No, it ended up in the Gulag and the secret police and all the other enforcers of morality. And in the meantime science invented instant obliteration.

Barbara   Which has what, exactly, to do with your English Faculty?

Delamere If there was nothing else, why wouldn't some people think that accuracy in writing, for example, the word or characterization or situation that most accurately depicted reality, and had the power to re-create the sensation of it – Well. Perhaps that accuracy had what amounted to a moral value.

Barbara   A moral value…

Delamere Was it art that could show us how to live? Could it describe a faulty society, and by implication suggest one that might work? Could it be our integrity, and restore our spirituality?

Barbara   Blimey.

Delamere Blimey indeed.

Barbara   But Hannah Vine thought it too airy-fairy?

Delamere I wouldn't say that airy-fairy is a precise analytical –

Barbara   Oh come on! But?

Delamere But she did have a notion of what would follow the lack of a grand narrative. The cruelty of the market would be presented as natural law and the little isms would claim to be the big story. As though a gender-neutral lavatory could end sub-Saharan drought.

Barbara That's a very patriarchal thing to say.

Delamere Don't you like men?

Barbara Do you like women?

Delamere I can never decide.

Barbara Women hate that in a man.

Delamere How would you describe your interviewing style, by the way?

Barbara When provoked? Swashbuckling.

Delamere There's something about me that provokes you?

Barbara You're a highbrow. I hate highbrows.

Delamere That's a very English reaction.

Barbara How can one lot of people say what's true or important?

Delamere Your readers, Miss Babs, are manipulated by corporate power that says that what sells the most is of necessity the best.

Barbara So my readers don't know art when they see it?

Delamere The only art that the market truly allows is advertising, which as we know is not art, because it does not seek the truth.

Barbara That was not an answer to my question.

Delamere No. But it's an insidiousness that cannot be denied.

Barbara This has become a bit of a ding-dong, hasn't it?

Delamere Yes.

Barbara I enjoy that.

Delamere So do I.

Barbara So did you fancy Hannah Vine or not?

Delamere Really, Miss Babs. Really, really, really.

Barbara You must let me buckle the occasional swash.

Delamere More like swashing a corroded buckle, I'd say.

Barbara Did you meet her socially?

Delamere Outside supervisions? No.

Barbara So you didn't know what she got up to?

Delamere Whatever it was, please consider that times change, and feelings with them.

Barbara She did have a boyfriend, actually.

Delamere In Cambridge?

Barbara For a year and a half. Bill Murdoch.

Delamere Bill Murdoch?

Barbara She never discussed him?

Delamere Of course not. Who was he?

Barbara He read Engineering.

Delamere Which college?

Barbara Selwyn. I found him. He's still alive.

Delamere Where?

Barbara He worked for oil companies.

Delamere He's retired?

Barbara To a golf course in Portugal.

Delamere I don't see Hannah Vine on a golf course.

Barbara Bill says he had a rival.

Delamere For Hannah?

Barbara An older man. It wasn't you, was it?

Exasperated.

What can he say?

　　　　　Bill agrees with you. He thinks it was a railway porter.

Delamere I'm speechless.

Barbara Hannah liked less clever men, Bill says, and even a bit of rough.

Delamere If that's to be the tone of your book, it won't do anyone any good.

Barbara Oh, dear. Are you going off me?

Delamere I'm not sure where I'm going.

Barbara No. Hannah's made me feel like that.

Delamere My supervisions were about set books, and I can't even remember now what those were.

Barbara But she did give off a female charge?

Delamere Green.

Barbara What?

Delamere Green. It can be a difficult colour to wear.

Barbara But she could.

Delamere Yes.

Barbara Why did you say that?

Delamere I don't know. I remembered.

Barbara What about her laugh?

Delamere Her laugh?

Barbara The other girls say she had a marvellous laugh.

Delamere Other girls?

Barbara In her year. The ones you supervised.

Delamere You've met them?

Barbara Mary Heath. Early retirement from the Foreign Office.

Delamere Mary Heath. A short person.

Barbara Tall.

Delamere Oh.

Barbara And the others. And Charlie Hawkins said the same.

Delamere Charlie Hawkins?

Barbara About her laugh.

Delamere Charlie Hawkins.

Barbara He knew her. He's a publisher. I tried to sell him the book but he wouldn't buy it. Can we talk now about Hannah's writings?

Delamere Why wouldn't he buy it?

Barbara I'll come to that. Bear with me.

Delamere *starts to speak.*

Then decides not to.

>Thank you. Hannah's books are all here, I observe. What would you say was their essence?

Delamere Heavens. Well. Feminist writers like Hannah are -

Barbara No. Sorry. I lost my thread. Before that. All those first friends agree that she never fudged. Never made exceptions in her own case. So many people's lives contradict their opinions, don't they?

Delamere They do.

Barbara Hers didn't, people say. She was unusually honest. Eventually the difficulty depressed her.

Delamere What?

Barbara People say.

Delamere People?

Barbara Ones she met in later life.

Delamere I don't know about her later life.

Barbara Some who say now that she was ahead of her time would have said then that she was a failure.

Delamere Miss Babs, writing must stand on its own. If we can't make a judgement without reference to the actual person we'd have to have Wordsworth in the room all the time.

Barbara But because of what happened Hannah is in the room, isn't she?

Delamere I'll continue, if I may, with what I was about to say.

Will she persist? No. Not this time. Go on.

Thank you. Well. Writers like Hannah are reformers, aren't they, and most reformers begin by describing what's outrageous and why it should be changed. Hannah thought that what should be changed was obvious, and so she began by

	examining what might never change. That is to say: instinct.
Barbara	Instincts can't be changed? They can't be tempered by society?
Delamere	Well. That would be the question. Wouldn't it?
Barbara	What do you think yourself?
Delamere	Do you feel that instincts have been tempered, when you turn on the television and see so many wars and hatreds?
Barbara	I think that in some societies women have far more freedom than in others. So that yes: instincts can be tempered.
Delamere	How quickly, would you say?
Barbara	Sometimes very quickly, when there's proper medicine and contraception.
Delamere	Which is why perhaps Hannah's books argue that efforts should be concentrated on those things, and that middle-class women in democratic societies had comparatively little to complain about.
Barbara	Yet they made the most noise.
Delamere	The most noise.
Barbara	Unlike working-class women stuck in tower blocks.
Delamere	Yes.
Barbara	Hannah's mother.
Delamere	And people they knew.
Barbara	But those lives did at least face reality.
Delamere	Yes: perhaps unfortunately.

Barbara Whereas middle-class empowerment, however important, may in some way have confused life and made relations between men and women more difficult.

Delamere Yes.

Barbara Is that idea what enraged people?

Delamere I suppose.

Barbara The famous moment on television.

Delamere Yes.

Barbara How would you describe it?

Delamere It was an early warning of today's level of cheap, barely educated, intolerant level of debate.

Barbara Strong words.

Delamere Which Hannah should have known to avoid because she did after all envisage it in her final book: a sort of touchy-feely politically correct consensus that is incapable of an accurate response to reality.

Barbara I promise that in my book you will be written as being more open-minded than you actually are.

Delamere What? Well. Really. Where were we? Yes.

Sets himself again.

Hannah was invited to give its annual lecture to a very serious learned society. In it, she compared the male sex drive and the maternal instinct. Each, she said, is as ruthless as the other, and each can be as positive or destructive as the other.

Barbara Destructive.

Delamere Instinctive relationships were, she thought, under-discussed by feminism: mothers and daughters, mothers and sons –

Barbara Mothers compete with daughters and can make or break sons.

Delamere As maybe. Fathers and sons. Fathers and daughters. Siblings. Her underlying theme was how instincts affect our more conscious feelings and decisions, and vice versa; and it was an observation in this context that was picked up by newspapers, as a result of which Hannah was invited to explain her ideas on TV.

Barbara The remark being that a few women move heaven and earth to have children, and when they do are jealous of them or don't want them.

Delamere Yes.

Barbara So…

Delamere Hannah went on the programme and talked about instincts in what was I suppose an academic sort of way, and so the interviewer said "Give me an example".

Barbara Which she did.

Delamere Yes.

Barbara "In the sexual act," she said, "it is the instinct of the man to dominate, and of the woman to submit, which is how she dominates the man in the end…"

Delamere Her exact words?

Barbara It's on YouTube.

Delamere Oh.

Barbara   You didn't know?

Delamere   Did she provoke the interviewer's outrage, do you think, or was she surprised?

Barbara   What's your opinion?

Delamere   I think that she was naïve about interviews.

Barbara   And that the interviewer was trying to get her to be less academic and more everyday.

Delamere   Yes.

Barbara   But what happened was that the interviewer couldn't stop her emotions.

Delamere   I expect you know her exact words, as well.

Barbara   "You talk about submission but what about the rest of us who are insulted and abused all day and made to feel like programmed robots because we bleed ...?"

Delamere   To which Hannah said: "So what do you think it would be like, a world with which women are satisfied?". And off the top of her head the interviewer couldn't say.

Barbara   Couldn't say? She'd gone ballistic.

Delamere   She said that the question was an insult and Hannah a traitor to all women everywhere. Which was the drama that stuck, of course.

Barbara   Headlines, worldwide.

Delamere   Awful.

Barbara   And the interviewer lost her job.

Delamere   Have you spoken to her?

Barbara   Yes.

He waits.

> She doesn't regret it. She was a divorced mother and thought that single childless Hannah was talking drivel.

Delamere What does she do now?

Barbara She's a life coach.

Delamere You've made that up.

Barbara I wish I had.

Delamere Oh dear. I did always wonder of course, if Hannah didn't ask the question out of simple curiosity. You know. What would the world be like? We might enjoy it.

Barbara Was that what you thought at the time?

Delamere At the time I thought that anyone with something serious to say was mad to say it on television.

Barbara It had a positive effect on Hannah's book sales. They rocketed.

Delamere Is that depressing, or not?

Barbara But a less good effect on Hannah. Some say it explains what happened.

Delamere What happened was an accident.

Barbara Why was Hannah single, in your opinion?

Delamere Well. Not everyone meets what used to be called the right person, do they?

Barbara You never married either, did you?

Delamere No.

Barbara   But you do have a daughter.

Delamere   Adopted, as it were, in later life.

Barbara   When did you last meet Hannah Vine?

Delamere   Meet her? Oh. Didn't I bump into her once? London bookshop. Blacklands Terrace.

Barbara   Before she'd written much?

Delamere   Anything. I couldn't put a date on it but didn't she ask me about some playwright? Edward Bond was it?

Barbara   Did you go to her funeral?

Delamere   As you surely know, there wasn't one.

Barbara   The memorial?

Delamere   No. Is this leading somewhere?

Barbara   I hope so.

Delamere   Where, if I might ask?

Barbara   Please bear with me.

Delamere   You've got some ghastly notion up your sleeve, haven't you?

Barbara   I wouldn't call it ghastly.

Delamere   A bee in your bonnet.

Barbara   Buzz buzz buzz.

Delamere   Is that buzzing why the publisher wouldn't buy your idea?

Is she a bit miffed that he's worked this out? Maybe.

I'm right. It is, isn't it?

Barbara   Charlie Hawkins. Yes. He wouldn't buy my premise.

Delamere   Which is, may I ask?

Barbara   I don't think that Hannah died when she's supposed to have done.

Delamere   What?

Barbara   She didn't commit suicide.

Delamere   I'm sure she didn't, but -

She waits.

She went to swim off a beach that has a notorious rip tide. She was swept away.

Barbara *waits.*

She left an unfinished book, for goodness sake.

Barbara   Where's the body?

Delamere   At peace, I hope, in the bosom of the ocean.

Again **Barbara** *waits.*

Do you put this claim to all your interviewees?

Barbara   I ask them to comment.

Delamere   On something so patently absurd?

Barbara   It's not absurd. It's legitimate. Even you in your ivory tower must know that various people claimed to have seen Hannah.

Delamere   After her death?

Barbara   Yes.

Delamere   What people?

Barbara   Readers. Admirers.

Delamere How many?

Barbara Five or six.

Delamere Ludicrous.

Barbara It was before websites or Twitter, of course. They wrote to feminist magazines.

Delamere Aren't there always such rumours about people who catch the imagination?

Barbara There can be. Then there was the student on a gap year who claimed to be Hannah's daughter.

Delamere Her daughter?

Barbara In Indonesia.

Delamere Indonesia?

Barbara She was on drugs. Written off as a fantasist. However.

Delamere However? Where was Hannah seen? Kathmandu I suppose.

Barbara The Isle of Wight.

Delamere The Isle of Wight?

Barbara On a walking holiday.

Delamere After she was dead?

Barbara Yes.

Delamere Did anyone challenge her?

Barbara It seems not.

Delamere Photographs?

Barbara One.

Delamere Very blurred, I imagine.

Barbara Very.

Delamere I mean, it's like who killed Jack Kennedy, isn't it? And as for appearances, there's a chap down the road who looks exactly like Saddam Hussein, but actually he's a Fellow in Classics at St Catherine's.

Barbara I'm sure. And I did dig up other sightings of Hannah.

Delamere Where were they?

Barbara On a bus in Edinburgh, and in a department store in Coventry.

Delamere Coventry. They could at least have come up with somewhere exotic.

Barbara Impossible. She couldn't travel.

Delamere What?

Barbara Well: how do you get a passport when you're dead and somebody else?

Delamere Really. You'll say next that the CIA organized Nine Eleven.

Barbara How do you know they didn't?

Delamere Oh for goodness sake.

Barbara Five days before she died Hannah made a will that left her future royalties to her old college.

Delamere I imagine they've done very well.

Barbara She also drew out most of her cash.

Delamere Really?

Barbara You didn't know?

Delamere Was it mentioned at the time?

Barbara Not really.

Delamere But you found out?

Barbara Sort of. No body, and no cash either.

Delamere You're not shallow, Miss Babs, and yet you'll write a shallow book. Why?

Barbara Well, suppose that in the archives of some stately home you found letters which proved that Shakespeare had performed fellatio on Ben Jonson. Would you publish?

Delamere Very foxy. Of course I'd publish.

Barbara So what's the difference?

Delamere Annotations, and in a learned journal.

Barbara Don't be silly.

Delamere Style. Understanding. Motive.

Barbara Elitism.

Delamere Is it?

Barbara I respect your world, Professor. But who cares about it? It's the past. It's dead.

Delamere Do you really believe that?

Barbara More or less.

Delamere I'm very sorry for you.

Barbara Why?

Delamere You don't even realise what you've lost.

Barbara Unlike Hannah.

Delamere What?

Barbara She did realise, didn't she? The world you described. No grand narrative. Lapsed everything. So why not a lapsed feminist. The world stinks, so leave it. Live a life that faces reality.

Delamere Preposterous.

Barbara Is it? Life today. Me me me. Money money money. Ratings ratings ratings. Politically correct rubbish that stops all serious enquiry. And for people who have nothing, there will be even less.

Delamere Well. Well, well. Now you sound like me.

Barbara Even if it isn't true it's a great story. She faked her death to make her life bearable. What a heroine!

Delamere And you'll write it whether or not.

Unexpectedly, she turns off the recorder.

Done? Interviewus interruptus?

Barbara As you said at the outcome, you never did know all about Hannah Vine.

Delamere No.

Barbara Did she know all about you?

Delamere Well, what she thought she knew could have been my alleged influence on her, I suppose.

Barbara Even if she thought: he's wonderful, but I mustn't become like that.

Delamere Even if.

Barbara But if she isn't dead, where is she? What's her name? What does she do? Or has she lived and died again, but this time for real?

Delamere Why ask me? If you've made up the question, why not make up the answers as well.

Barbara That's just what I thought. I've done it before, after all. But the more I look, the more I know that my theory has to be true.

Delamere You know.

Barbara I know. No single reason. I just know. I can't prove it, of course. Not yet. But when I can I'd like to talk to you again.

Delamere When? Don't you mean if?

Barbara If, then. If I return can we do that? Or will you deny me entry?

Delamere Despite a myriad of misgivings, to do so would be foolish, I think, as well as discourteous.

Barbara Thank you.

Delamere Is there at this moment, any more to be said?

Barbara No. I don't think so.

Delamere Perfect.

Barbara On the other hand.

Delamere What?

Barbara There is one thing that interviewees have begun to want to know.

Delamere What?

Barbara Will I sell what I write to the films or television?

Delamere Will you?

Barbara I'll give it a try.

Delamere As a drama?

Barbara I've done it before.

Delamere So what's the question?

Barbara Could I stop them putting you in it?

Delamere Of course. Good heavens. Could you?

Barbara I shouldn't think so.

Delamere Why not?

Barbara Well. You really existed. Didn't you?

Delamere Yes. If you put it that way. I suppose I did. Why don't I don my muffler, and see you to the garden gate?

They go.

Scene Two   The Same   Evening

Delamere *and* ***Clementine*** *burst in. She is late 20s, slim and beautiful, but awry. She is panicked and trying to breathe.*

Clementine Help. Help me. I can't – I need – oh God – oh –

Delamere It's in your hand.

Clementine Your fault – What did you say? – I can't –

Delamere In your hand, Clementine.

Clementine What?

But it is. The brown paper bag.

Oh…

She blows into it.

The classic stand-by for a panic attack.

Deep breaths and blow.

> Oh…

Breathe and blow.

> Oh…

She's calmer.

Her breathing slows.

It becomes more natural.

It's the quiz. Time for the quiz.

Delamere Clem. In all conscience.

Clementine No.

He would protest but she stops him.

She grabs the remote and turns the TV on.

> Be normal. Do what we always do. Watch the quiz. Come on. Beat the contestants.

With reluctance he complies.

Delamere Christopher Columbus. Oh, come on. These people don't know anything. Santa Maria. Not that anyone knows anything since the school curriculum was shot to pieces. Nina. Pinta. Who did that? Was it Labour or the Tories?

Clementine Both.

Delamere Both.

Clementine They both feel guilty about the past, so how could they teach it properly?

Delamere The Sahara Desert. Margaret Thatcher didn't feel guilty.

Clementine Margaret Thatcher hated learning for its own sake. It could lead to economic wet dreams.

Delamere Timbuctoo. Lower middle class, you see. Corner shop owners. Bedrocks of philistinism. The Gambia River. Mungo Park. Clementine, we really must discuss what's happened today.

Clementine No

Reluctantly he gives her more time.

Delamere How much have we won so far?

Clementine Two million in the last three weeks.

Delamere Would that solve our problems?

Clementine If it was real. So do it for real. Go on the telly for real.

Delamere They want youth. Sexy ignorance.

Clementine Lose on looks, gain on the sympathy factor.

Delamere I'm too proud. I can't afford to lose.

Clementine We have lost. Years ago.

Delamere On a TV quiz one night and dinner in Hall the next? I'd be a laughing stock. Easy. Playwrights. Terence Rattigan. Whiting. Edward –

A thought stops him in his tracks.

Clementine What's the matter?

Delamere Nothing. Edward Bond. Everything.

He snaps off the television.

Silence.

He tries to return to another topic.

Delamere Then in the name of social engineering governments made universities lower their standards and take more people.

Clementine And at the same time they cut their funding.

Delamere But nobody notices. They're all ignorant together.

Clementine Okay. Fine. But you must realise what it was that upset me.

Delamere I do. I apologise.

Clementine You knew about this biographer woman for a whole week but said nothing.

Delamere I wanted to be sure of the strength of her.

Clementine Sure. To protect us. You. Me. Whatever.

Delamere Yes.

Clementine Very well. Can we start again? Go back fifteen minutes? I've just come home. I'm still in my coat. I'd had my nightmare about Rupert dying and I remembered it all day.

Delamere Don't imagine his death, Clementine. Imagine him here, and laughing.

Clementine I know. I do try to do that. So what's her name?

Delamere Miss Babs. It could just as well have been Miss Boobs.

Clementine Boobs who?

Delamere Sorry. Barbara Cavalier.

Clementine   Barbara Cavalier?

Delamere   It can't be her real name, can it? Surely not. Yet she's curiously honest.

Clementine   Oh, Delamere!

Delamere   What?

Clementine   How out of touch you are.

Delamere   You mean you know who she is?

Clementine   Of course I know.

Delamere   You've not read her books, have you?

Clementine   I've read the one about the rock singer who died with one woman underneath him and another on top, and I've flicked the photos in the one about whatshername.

Delamere   Whatshername?

Clementine   Still alive. The cosmetics heiress who's a vampire.

Delamere   My God. Are these books in the house?

Clementine   Airports, darling. Devour on the plane and bin on arrival. How much does she know?

Delamere   She's a sniffer.

Clementine   Did you try to say earlier that she'll come back?

Delamere   Yes.

Clementine   When?

Delamere   She was very taken by your wedding photograph.

Clementine   You didn't think to hide it?

Delamere   No.

Clementine Why not?

Delamere I forgot.

Clementine You forgot? Damn it to hell, Delamere, if she realised that I'm the image of my mother, and if she recognised the outside of the college chapel, she can be on internet genealogical sites in two clicks.

Delamere I know. Bingo.

Clementine Bingo?

Delamere I'm sorry.

Clementine It wasn't deliberate, was it?

Delamere Deliberate?

Clementine Take a chance. Leave it to fate. See what she knows.

Delamere Maybe.

Clementine What?

Delamere I'm old, Clementine, and we've hidden things. We haven't faced them. You didn't even tell your own husband. Who are we? Who's Hannah Vine?

Clementine Stop it. Shut up. Where's my –?

It's in her hand.

Blow.

Breathe.

Sorry. I must remember I'm not a child. This woman. Where is she? She'll come back?

Delamere At any time.

Clementine Seriously?

Delamere Seriously. She knows.

Clementine She said so?

Delamere No.

Clementine So how can you be sure?

Delamere Integrity.

Clementine What?

Delamere She's a dealer in fakes who's recognized a real masterpiece.

Clementine So what should we do?

Delamere What do you want to do?

Clementine Take the money and run.

Delamere Run?

Clementine What else is there?

Delamere Old fashioned grit. Say nothing. Do nothing.

Clementine I've tried that.

Delamere Have you?

Clementine More or less. When I was eighteen and told that my mother who died when I was a kid was somebody else altogether and that – Then I tried going to pieces, as you know, and was put together again by you and my amazing Rupert who I loved and loved, and that was easy. You'd taught me to speak proper and I could always stand straight like – What was her name?

Delamere Hannah Vine.

Clementine	Hannah Vine. So lo and behold. Grit. I was the officer's wife. And I loved the idea of the regiment. Service. To die for something serious. Which Rupert – I mean at the time I was a mess and ignored Tony Blair's untruthful war, but it led to – Well, you and I tried Afghanistan from afar, didn't we, and Rupert trod on a mine and – He was in three large pieces, wasn't he? Isn't that what somebody let slip? He was blown into three –
Delamere	Clementine –
Clementine	Three pieces. Oh fuck. Sorry, I was in a million pieces but you've been putting me together again. Is it hereditary?
Delamere	What?
Clementine	Coming to pieces.
Delamere	You aren't in pieces.
Clementine	Was my father sex on legs?
Delamere	What?
Clementine	That was it, wasn't it? Working class sex on legs.
Delamere	I never met him.
Clementine	Delamere, if there's a decision to be made, if our lives are going to be splattered across tabloids and airport bookstalls. I need to know what she was like. Actually like.
Delamere	I've told you a thousand times.
Clementine	No you haven't. What did she want? Does any daughter know her mother? I mean actually, between her legs and what – You have to tell me what she was like.

Delamere You know what she was like.

Clementine No.

Delamere You do.

Clementine No.

Delamere You know because I've told you.

Clementine You've tried to tell me. But can you?

Delamere Yes. Of course I – No. I'm sorry. I – No, I don't think I could ever have told you. I must have – I was in love with her. So I invented her. Sorry.

Clementine Oh dear…

Then out of their silence she goes to pour a whisky.

Delamere Should you?

Clementine No.

Downs it. Pours another.

Delamere You don't still do cocaine, do you? Ever? When you go to hear those bands in the pub, or – No.

Clementine No.

Delamere Hannah was into cannabis, you know. She always knew where to find it.

Clementine Didn't you?

Delamere Me? Lord, no. I was too boring.

Clementine Golly. You never told me that before. Why not?

Delamere I didn't want to justify your excesses.

Clementine Very stand-in parental.

Delamere In some Ritz hotel somewhere Hannah just walked up to the concierge and asked him.

Clementine Helpful?

Delamere Very. He got on the telephone.

Clementine You should have married her.

Delamere She wouldn't have me.

Clementine Any further thoughts on why not?

Delamere She was endlessly pestered, of course, by ridiculous macho men.

Clementine That was the reason?

Delamere No.

Clementine Then why?

Delamere You've asked this a million times. Why do people? No reason and every reason.

Clementine Feelings.

Delamere Feelings. Of course, and as I'm telling you for the million and first time, when she was my pupil our relationship was perforce clandestine, and somehow it stayed that way.

Clementine Well it's more exciting, isn't it?

Delamere Venice was bad for us, but we always did well in Vienna.

Clementine It must have cost a fortune.

Delamere She made a fortune.

Clementine She paid?

Delamere At first I did. Later we ran a kitty.

Clementine She did that on the Isle of Wight.

Delamere You told me.

Clementine Her mother had done it, she said, and I said 'Why can't we see your Mummy and she said "She's dead". D'you think she was?

Delamere I don't know.

Clementine You never met her.

Delamere No.

Clementine Did people recognize Hannah?

Delamere Later, you mean? When we were together? I've told you. No. She wore wigs.

Clementine My God. Why don't I?

Delamere Then one day she said "I can't do this any longer" and to my surprise I said "Neither can I."

Clementine So you didn't.

Delamere No.

Clementine Whisky?

Delamere Why not?

Clementine *pours it for him.*

Clementine So you never saw her again and she became more and more controversial and one day you read that she was dead.

Delamere Then years later she came to the door. A dowdy working-class woman in an anorak. Face chalk white. Death in it.

Clementine The cancer.

Delamere "Jack's dead," she said. "It killed him when the factory closed. He lost his meaning in life." I said, "Who are you? What are you talking about?" Then my God but I saw it was her and she said "I want you to look after Clementine."

Clementine So we moved in.

Delamere I told people she was my sister and they believed me. D'you remember?

Clementine You told me later.

Delamere Amazing, really.

Clementine The one time you did life better than scholarship.

Delamere Yes.

Clementine One thing I never asked you.

Delamere What?

Clementine Did you fuck her?

Delamere What?

Clementine Here. Those last months.

Delamere No.

Clementine Why not? Sorry. Cancer of the cervix. Don't ask. Is that hereditary as well?

He won't answer. What can he say?

Sorry. But you did talk to her. You did ask "Why?" and she did say "The day before I killed Hannah Vine I did want to phone you to ask your opinion. But I didn't because I was afraid you'd persuade me not to do it."

Delamere She didn't phone because by that time we'd said it all. She said she'd wanted to because for a woman love's never as cut and dried as men would like it to be, is it?

98   Hannah Vine

Clementine   Did Jack know who she was and not care?

Delamere   Maybe.

Clementine   She always had paperback poetry. He never looked at it.

Delamere   What did he read?

Clementine   The evening paper.

No more to say, except -

Delamere   Miss Babs tried to sell the idea to Charlie Hawkins.

Clementine   Our Charlie Hawkins?

Delamere   Ours.

Clementine   What happened?

Delamere   He didn't believe her, so he turned her down.

Clementine   But he warned you?

Delamere   He did.

Clementine   How long ago?

Delamere   Months.

Clementine   Why didn't you tell me?

Delamere   You were in a mess.

Clementine   You're a dictatorial old patriarch, Delamere, d'you know that?

Delamere   Yes. Think of me as the Colonel of the regiment.

Clementine   Colonel? I suppose you came on to Miss Babs as some old-fashioned literary fuddy-duddy?

Delamere	I did my best.
Clementine	Was she deceived?
Delamere	She was while it lasted.
Clementine	Delamere I'm just a tight-lipped military widow who does what passes for work in a charity shop, for fuck's sake. You'll have to be more explicit.
Delamere	You're too young to swear all the time.
Clementine	Well, I blew my education, didn't I?
Delamere	It didn't stop you reading, however.
Clementine	Do you think I could write?
Delamere	Write? Write what?
Clementine	You know: stuff.
Delamere	Have you tried?
Clementine	In secret. All the time.
Delamere	You've given up on being the front girl in a band?
Clementine	Just tell me more about Charlie chocolate-pudding Hawkins.
Delamere	Fiction? Poetry? What? When can I read it?
Clementine	Hawkins.
Delamere	Of course. Sorry. I phoned him.
Clementine	When?
Delamere	As soon as Miss Babs left the house.

The doorbell rings.

Clementine	Did you order a taxi?
Delamere	Dinner in Hall? Not tonight.

Clementine Then it's her: she's back. What did Charlie say?

Delamere I had to explain everything, you understand. How we've hidden what we've hidden for all these years. He was miffed. Until he weighed it, that is.

Doorbell again.

Delamere We did always know that one day there would have to be a choice.

Clementine Which is mine, you have always insisted.

Delamere Yes.

Clementine So what did Charlie say? Any money you like and what are your terms?

Doorbell again.

She begins to panic.

Delamere *gets up and goes to answer.*

Her paper bag.

Does she need it?

Not quite.

She manages to be composed.

And is, of course, most striking in appearance.

Delamere *comes back with* **Barbara**.

Delamere Clementine. This is Miss Cavalier of whom we spoke earlier. Miss Cavalier – this is Clementine.

Barbara Call me Babs.

Clementine Miss Boobs. Babs. Sorry.

Barbara Wow. Hannah Vine's daughter. In spirit and absolute appearance.

Clementine   You'll say next that you fancy me.

Barbara   I do.

Clementine   Really?

Barbara   Really.

Clementine   Madly?

Barbara   Madly.

They stare at each other: serious appraisals.

Delamere   My God. Love's lightning bolt, much written about, but seldom seen.

Clementine   What?

Barbara   What?

Delamere   Aroused emotions, that change everything.

Clementine   Everything?

Barbara   Everything.

Delamere   Whisky, Miss Babs, after what I'm sure were your extreme exertions on the internet?

Barbara   Perfect. Thank you.

Clementine   Ice? Water? Twist of lemon?

Barbara   Not a cocktail girl as well?

Clementine   Shake me and see.

Barbara   I think I have.

Clementine   Never use the same ice twice.

She goes to get the drink. **Delamere** *is a wry spectator.*

Barbara   Sorry. Unexpected. A mega-intrusion of the personal.

Delamere Not at all.

Barbara You're not surprised?

Delamere I don't think so.

Barbara Why not?

Delamere Well. You were already in love with the idea of Hannah Vine.

Barbara So you won't lie to me now, will you?

Delamere Did I lie to you before?

Barbara London bookshop? Edward Bond?

Delamere Yes: well: you realised that Edward Bond flourished some time after Hannah left the university, which meant that I had continued to see her and –

Stops. Shrugs. What else is there to say?

Barbara And a positive Watergate of denials about everything else. On the other hand, why didn't you hide the photo?

Delamere Old age. I forgot.

Barbara You forgot?

Clementine *gives* **Barbara** *her whisky.*

Clementine Cheers. Of course. It's like what happened to his Maserati.

Barbara He had a Maserati?

Clementine Old age. Forgot he was in top gear. Wrote it off.

Barbara Speed?

Delamere Speed.

Barbara Disqualified?

Delamere	Got away with it.
Clementine	London lawyers. Chin chin.

*But **Barbara** just stares.*

	I say. There's not a fly in your ice-cube, is there?
Barbara	You're very flippant and sure of yourselves. What's happened?
Clementine	Happened?
Barbara	Something's happened? What's happened?

They glance at each other but say nothing.

	You've decided something. You've discussed it and made up your minds.
Delaware	I've decided nothing.
Barbara	You've decided nothing?
Clementine	She was my mother. So it's my decision.
Barbara	To talk or not to talk?
Clementine	More than that.
Barbara	More? What more? Professor?
Delamere	Miss Babs, our lives have been private.
Barbara	If you think that you can stop curiosity about history you can't. You must know that.
Delamere	Photographers in the driveway aren't curiosity about history.
Barbara	Yes they are. Of course they are. So am I.
Clementine	How can you be, when half of what you write's invented?
Barbara	So what would you call that: literary fiction?

Delamere   Very good, Miss Babs. Very witty.

Clementine   Oh, come on, Delamere, you can do a better put-down than that.

Delamere   Can I? Of course I can. Yes. Literary fiction is a false definition imposed by publishers' sales reps upon work they think too difficult to promote.

Barbara   I love sales reps. I send them hampers at Christmas.

Delamere   Whereas there once really was a world in which John Murray burned Lord Byron's letters.

Barbara   John Murray?

Delamere   He died in 1843. He was a publisher.

Barbara   Byron's.

Delamere   Yes.

Barbara   Letters burned to avoid a scandal.

Delamere   Supposedly.

Barbara   What a loss to vulgar curiosity.

Delamere   At least it wasn't money-grabbing.

Barbara   Not to mention scholarship.

Clementine   She's clocking up points, Delamere. Do admit.

Barbara   You know what this is, don't you?

Delamere   What?

Barbara   Chaff between instant friends.

Clementine   Chaff.

Barbara   We could go on like this for yonks.

Clementine   We could. Of course we could. So?

Barbara	So I'm part of it.
Clementine	It?
Barbara	Hannah Vine. Your lives. The entire dilemma.
Delamere	Well. Yes. I suppose there is a chance that you may be.
Barbara	At the very least you owe me some answers. At the best I can share the disarray.
Delamere	True. You may very well have to.
Clementine	Delamere, setting aside for the moment the unnerving fact that Miss Babs and I seem to fancy each other like mad, has something happened here of which I am unaware?
Delamere	If we answer the questions we'll find out.
Clementine	Straight answers, you mean? No disinformation?
Delamere	Certainly not yet.
Barbara	Not yet?
Delamere	Just ask me what you want to know.
Barbara	Very difficult when I can't trust a word you say. But did you know at the time that Hannah's death was faked?
Delamere	No. We went out of each other's lives for many years. Until she needed me to help Clementine, in fact.
Barbara	But you were the older man at Cambridge.
Clementine	Russian spies. All the way.
Barbara	What?

Clementine A joke.

Barbara Why did she ask Delamere to help you?

Clementine Dad's sister was in Canada. I didn't fancy it. D'you think I should have?

Barbara How old were you?

Clementine How old was I?

Delamere Ten?

Clementine Thereabouts.

Barbara Did you know about Delamere?

Clementine Her teacher, she said. I thought she meant at school.

Barbara Were you happy?

Clementine Here?

Barbara Before. Before Jack died.

Clementine Very.

Barbara Were they?

Clementine They were Mum and Dad.

Barbara But were they happy?

Clementine Yes. I mean, I was a kid, so I've no idea, really, have I? I just know how they made it seem to me.

Barbara *waits.*

What I remember best was when I was a bit older, and by then Dad was ill.

Barbara What was it like after that?

Clementine It was the two of us.

Again **Barbara** *waits for a moment.*

Barbara Did she tell you that she was dying herself?

Does **Clementine** *need her paper bag?*

No. She will do without it.

Clementine I don't think I listened. Did I? We just came here to live.

Another pause.

Clementine *is steady.*

Barbara The question must be, and we've all asked it, haven't we: did she kill herself and then meet your father? Or meet your father and then decide to die?

Clementine I've wondered how I could do it, you know. Die, and come back as the person I think I want to be. Wow.

Barbara What's the answer?

Clementine I don't know.

Barbara She never told you?

Clementine No.

Barbara Do you know?

Delamere No.

Barbara Why not?

Delamere Why would I?

Barbara You're a scholar.

Delamere I was her lover. Would I want her to die for another man?

Barbara How did you discover who she was?

Clementine She left me a letter with Delamere. Read aged eighteen.

Barbara You didn't destroy it?

Clementine He didn't.

Barbara Why not?

Delamere Would you want me to destroy your last wishes?

Silence.

Clementine What I did always know, of course, was where Mum and Dad met each other.

Barbara Where?

Clementine In a cinema queue.

Barbara What was the film?

Clementine They forgot.

Barbara Forgot?

Clementine They were smitten. They went off somewhere.

Barbara She told you this?

Clementine Yes.

Barbara My God. He must have been – What was he like? Did he know who she was?

Clementine He taught me to play shove ha'penny.

Barbara Oh no. Like the Probation Officer.

Clementine Who?

Delamere A person in Miss Cavalier's past.

Barbara Council offices. He played on his office table.

Clementine Well: it was another world.

Barbara	It was. Have you still got Hannah's letter? What did it say?
Clementine	It said to ask Delamere to tell me who she used to be.
Barbara	Why did she want you to know?
Clementine	To pass on what she thought she'd learned, I suppose. Isn't that what mothers do?
Barbara	What had she learned?
Delamere	She left it to us to decide.
Clementine	All it's done is screw me up, of course, but at the same time –

Stops.

What?

What at the same time?

Barbara	At the same time? What? Did she want the world to know?
Clementine	I can't make up my mind what's best for her.
Barbara	What's best for her? She's dead.
Clementine	No she isn't, and that's the problem. She's living in other people's ideas of her, and so will we if something's published.
Barbara	You can manipulate what other people think.
Clementine	That's exactly what's horrible.
Barbara	Horrible? She's an inspiration. Why else d'you think I want to write about her?

Unexpected. They stare at her.

> I seem to have finished my whisky.

Clementine You're at home. Help yourself.

She goes. Turns back. But does not drink.

> The meaning of life. No narrative. Surely shopping can't be all there is.

Clementine *makes the sign of raising her glass.*

> Cheers.

Barbara	How did Hannah Vine find the courage?
Delamere	She always had courage. What she found was doubt.
Barbara	I suppose that's why I hated it when you fobbed me off.
Delamere	In which case I apologise: it was never about trying to dismiss you.
Barbara	It wasn't? Then what was it about?
Clementine	It's about whether we're John Murray or a sales rep.
Barbara	Whether you tell or shut up, you mean?
Clementine	Well it's not even that, is it, really? It's could I live with the intrusion and the money or would it screw me up worse than I am? Or would not taking it screw me up more?
Barbara	Money?
Delamere	Your research is excellent Miss Babs but you missed something very important.
Barbara	What?
Delamere	Charlie Hawkins.
Clementine	Chocolate Charlie.

Barbara You know him?

Delamere He was my student. Double First. I had high hopes of him but it was Hannah who said "No, no. He's just an amusing careerist." Correct as usual.

Barbara He knew Hannah Vine because of you?

Delamere Me.

Barbara Did he know what she did and about Clementine?

Delamere Of course not.

Barbara But he warned you about me?

Delamere He did.

Barbara So you were ready.

Delamere After you left I called him, and had to tell him everything, of course. More or less.

Clementine More or less?

Barbara What did he say?

Delamere He'll give us double any other offer.

Clementine Us?

Delamere You and me.

Clementine Up front?

Delamere It would only be the start, he reckons.

Barbara You can't do that. You can't do a deal with Charlie Hawkins.

Delamere Why not?

Barbara Principles? Massive betrayal of?

Delamere Doesn't Hannah deserve a full scholarly biography?

Barbara Charlie wants the dirt like everyone else.

Delamere Well, we have that as well, don't we? Photos. Diaries. Love letters.

Barbara I'm sorry but I think you're fucking outrageous.

Clementine And it's for me to decide, actually.

Delamere Of course. But in view of Miss Babs it's more pressing.

Barbara You mean without me you'd have done nothing?

Clementine Well. I'd have agonized and he'd have left his archive to the college library.

Delamere Subject to embargo.

Barbara Embargo? You're fantasists. Why am I obsessed by you?

Delamere Because we don't want to live your modern life.

Barbara I'm not sure that modern life is mine any more. For which I blame Hannah Vine. Who'll write your Charlie Hawkins book?

Clementine If there is one? Me.

Barbara You?

Clementine Me.

Barbara All right. All right. I'll make a proposal. If you love me and come to live with me I won't write anything. Or, if you want, we'll write a book together.

Clementine No.

Barbara	Why not?
Clementine	Well, we know we fancy each other so we can go to Las Vegas if you like. Give it a whirl on a waterbed. New thing for me. See if it helps. But no writing.
Barbara	Why not?
Clementine	You don't do it properly.
Barbara	I don't write properly?
Clementine	No.
Barbara	Who cares?
Clementine	Me. I do write properly.
Barbara	But people don't read properly anymore. Do they?
Delamere	No. So how should we respond. That's my quandary.
Barbara	The quandary is how can Miss Cocktail Shaker say that she doesn't want to be written about and then insist that she'll write it herself?
Clementine	Think of it as a pre-nup agreement.
Delamere	Pre what?
Barbara	Nup. Tabloid language. Nuptual.
Delamere	She's asking you to marry her?
Barbara	If there's any proposing it'll be done by me. How do I know you can write properly?
Clementine	Because I can.
Barbara	Who says so?
Clementine	Me.

Barbara	Can she?
Delamere	I've no idea.
Barbara	What?
Clementine	Actually, none of us have eaten, have we?
Barbara	Eaten?
Clementine	I made a minestrone before I left this morning. Heat up job.
Barbara	Oh shut up. And fuck Charlie Hawkins. Fuck him.
Delamere	Many have.
Barbara	You're a sham. You just want to keep up your lifestyle. I don't wonder Hannah Vine gave up on you.
Clementine	Actually they were a perfect match.
Delamere	So long as we kept apart, that is.
Clementine	I think I'll go and be a housewife.

She goes into the kitchen.

A somewhat stunned silence.

Barbara	This is happening, isn't it? I'm not in some cyber version of an editorial conference, am I?
Delamere	We wanted to be private, you see. We never needed the noise and the money. All we needed was to live with our feelings.
Barbara	Is she like Hannah? Is that what her mother was like?
Delamere	If I could secure casting approval, who do you think should play me in the movie?

Barbara	Henry Irving.
Delamere	He's dead.
Barbara	I know.
Delamere	Would you really take her to Las Vegas?
Barbara	Would she go?
Delamere	Who knows about love, Miss Babs?
Barbara	Not me, it seems. Not any more, thank God. Did Hannah Vine?
Delamere	She experienced it. Isn't that enough?
Barbara	No. I don't know. Yes.
Delamere	Which takes us, of course, into another area of debate.
Barbara	What?
Delamere	Love, Miss Babs, is a subject addressed more by my dead poets than by your feminist writers. Why is that, do you think?

Clementine *appears, wearing an apron. She is upset but in control.*

Clementine	Delamere, I need my mother to help me to decide what to do.
Delamere	She isn't here, darling. She went out, and came back as someone else. Don't you remember?
Clementine	Why did she do that?
Delamere	I don't know. She never told me. She always assumed that because I loved her I would know.
Clementine	I'll wrap a baguette in foil and pop it in the oven.

She returns to the kitchen. **Barbara** *wants to follow.*

Barbara   Darling, let me help you, or at least –

But she thinks the better of it.

Sorry. Wait to be entitled. Did I really offer not to write a book? If she loves me why would she stop me? Do I want to answer that question?

Delamere   No. You want to be resurrected as somebody else.

Barbara   And my publisher's advance is non-returnable. What about you?

Delamere   Me? I'm an old fool. I want the whole world to be the way it was.

Barbara   You mean nobody writes anything until after we're all dead, and I look after Clementine somewhere in the country?

Delamere   I had a similar sort of dream myself, once, about the famous feminist writer Hannah Vine.

Barbara   What happened?

Delamere   In the end? You arrived.

Barbara   Oh dear.

Delamere   Not at all. You provided the opportunity.

Barbara   You mean – you always wanted it to be public?

He would weigh his reply but **Clementine** *returns.*

Clementine Come on. Ditch your whisky glasses. Soup's up. And I've made some very good family decisions.

The End

Steerforth in Italy

CHARACTERS

in order of appearance

Henri	a minor diplomat
David	a shorthand reporter and aspiring writer
James	a dissolute rentier
Emily	his young mistress
Littimer	a manservant

SETTINGS

Prologue:	The Customs Post at Pietra Sante
One:	Lodgings in Naples
Two:	The same
Three:	The Borghese Gardens in Rome
Four:	A terrace in Fiesole
Epilogue:	The Customs Post at Pietra Sante

Prologue **Pietra Sante** **1840**

The waiting room in the customs post on the Tuscan side of the border with the Papal States.

Henri *is in his 50s, smallish, fat, ugly in his own estimation, yet spiky, charismatic, world-weary and at the same time curious.*

He is in indifferent health but in command of himself, a minor diplomat returning to his post. He wears little steel spectacles to read.

There is a commotion outside. He takes it in but returns to his book. Commotions are not after all infrequent, and this is Italy – heat, light, languor and ancient knowledge.

Then **David** *bursts in. He is English and not very old, maybe 20 even. He is overdressed for the heat but he has been travelling.*

He is agitated, and argues with someone outside.

David Non, je ne suis – je suis très angry and insulted and – wrong language, dammit – sono incenso, sono – this is entirely contrary to all international convention and law, and what's more sono un British citoyen and I won't stand for it.

He sees **Henri** *and feels foolish.*

Sir.

Henri Monsieur.

David *realises what is happening outside.*

David No. No.

Henri Lui donnez un pourboire.

David What?

Henri Coins. How did you say?

Snaps his finger for the English word.

Remembers it.

> Change. Give him your change.

David   That's a bribe.

Henri   Of course.

David   British Customs Officers are incorruptible, and Britons do not grease palms.

Henri *is watching.*

Is he cynical about English probity?

> This is insufferable.

David *goes outside.*

Henri *notes what is happening.*

Then he returns to his book.

David *re-appears.*

He looks at **Henri**, *then talks to the man outside.*

> Thank you. Grazie. I trust that everything will now be re-packed exactly as it was before you opened it.

He turns back in.

Now what should he do?

Henri *indicates. Why not sit down?*

> Thank you.

David *sits. he must acknowledge* **Henri**, *he realises.*

> Thank you, sir. Your command of our language seems almost proficient.

Prologue

Henri I have long considered the English to be the most barbarous people in the whole world.

David You've what?

Henri Henri Beyle. Consul of the French Government in Civitavecchia. At your service.

David David Copperfield.

Shake hands.

David *sits again.*

Civitavecchia?

Henri Civitavecchia.

David You're travelling north.

Henri North.

Silence.

Et vous-même?

David What? Oh. South. I think near Naples.

Henri Naples.

David *nods. then he gets up. looks out.*

David Wrong things in the wrong trunk.

He sighs and shrugs.

I must seek the amusing side, I suppose.

He's ill at ease.

He mops his face.

He sits again.

Henri *picks his moment.*

Henri Forgive me. But did you say Copperfield?

David	Coppperfield.
Henri	And you are not positive of your destination?
David	No.

He does not enlarge.

*So **Henri** must ask.*

Henri	Does this – forgive me – is this the indication that you seek a young lady?
David	How do you know that?
Henri	My dear young man you show too much the symptoms.
David	Symptoms?
Henri	Obsession. Restfulness. An idée fixe. Rapid breath. Your lips move as you orate yourself.
David	Orate myself?
Henri	You are in love, I think.
David	Am I? I mean, is that how I seem? I mean, I – Thank you.

Takes a breath. He must pull himself together.

	How wise you are, sir. How little I serve myself, to be so agitated.
Henri	The smallest tremor can release the avalanche.
David	I'm not in love myself, sir, and yet my mission concerns love: the defilement and betrayal of love, and the havoc of indulgent sensuality…

Henri *snaps his book shut.*

Henri	My God…

David	I have come to rescue a young woman, and to take her home.
Henri	She was abducted?
David	Seduced.
Henri	Seduced.
David	Nay, she was ravaged, and I will assist her to expunge her shame.

Well! Thinks **Henri**. *And waits.*

David *cannot stop himself now.*

> When I was a child, sir, I had a nurse, a simple woman from the fisher-folk whose name was Peggoty, and that woman had a brother, and that brother a daughter named Emily, my sometime playmate from another social class, a child of purity and innocence.

He stops, as if seeing her before his eyes.

He is almost in tears.

> Seduced, sir. Lured from her home by promises of I know not what.

Henri	And the seducer?
David	A man of birth, means, education, charm and boredom. And of selfishness. Of callousness. And what is worse, he does not mean to lack scruples. He simply cannot help it. My suspicion is that it pains him greatly.
Henri	So you know him.
David	He was my dearest friend.
Henri	As is often the case.

David	What?
Henri	Je vous en prie. Continue.
David	He was my protector when I was at school. My hero. The person I wanted to be like; and for him to like me, of course. To take me with him into his magical world.
Henri	But he took the girl.
David	They met because of me.
Henri	You feel responsible.
David	Alas.
Henri	They ran away.
David	Ran away.
Henri	They came to Italy?
David	France. Belgium. The Rhine. Switzerland.
Henri	The St Bernard.
David	The St Bernard into Italy. There were letters.
Henri	From the young woman?
David	They begged forgiveness. They grew unhappier in tone.
Henri	He abandoned her?
David	Not yet. Not so far as we know.

Silence.

Her uncle came to look for them but he was a poor man with no money. So when I made some myself I resumed the quest.

Prologue 125

Henri	This happened some years ago?
David	A few.
Henri	What is the name of your friend?
David	Steerforth. James Steerforth. He has a dishonest manservant named Littimer.
Henri	Littimer…
David	You know them?
Henri	I'm a consul. I issue passports. My agents tell me stories.
David	You do know them. Great heavens. Where are they? What …
Henri	My dear young man…
David	… more do you know? How can I…?

David *stops.*

He has pushed impolitely, he realises.

Henri	All that I say is: you have struck a bell.
David	Don't you mean rung a chime? No. I apologise. Sorry. Why should you know him?
Henri	Yet may I ask you a question? Did your Englishman like the opera?
David	Opera? Why would he like the opera?
Henri	Opera singers, maybe.
David	I don't know. I don't think so. Oh. You don't mean fast women, do you?
Henri	A memory of someone else, perhaps. So many English come to Italy, you know…
David	Yes.

David *would ask more, but sees that there is action outside.*

> Your horses. They seem to be ready.

Henri   Thank you.

He gathers himself to go.

David   So I should enquire at the opera houses, you think.

Henri   Maybe. Why not?

David   Thank you.

Henri   May I advise you?

David   I'm sure I need it.

Henri   En garde. Italy has always changed its invaders.

David   But isn't villainy always villainy, in any language?

Henri *shrugs. He has seen a great deal in his time.*

Henri   Adieu Mr Copperfield. Bon voyage. Bonne chance.

David   Thank you.

Henri *goes.*

David *would ask more.*

> Sir, if I might…

But **Henri** *is too far away.*

> Thank you. Merci. Grazie.

He tries to be more resolute.

At least he has a hint of information.

Then he realises that they are ready for him.

>Yes. Baggage ready. I'm coming.

David *goes.*

Scene One   **Naples**   **1837**

James Steerforth's lodgings. Afternoon heat. **James** *reads.* **Emily** *drifts in.*

She has been lying down and wears her négligée.

Once she would not have had to wait. He would have gone after her and made love.

She idles about.

He looks but returns to his book.

Emily   James…

James   Mm…?

She flashes him.

Emily   Boo!

Shuts her gown.

It hasn't worked.

>Sorry.

James   What?

Emily   I'm stupid.

James   No, you aren't.

Emily   No.

She thinks about it.

>But I'm still not a lady, am I?

James *is bored by this question.*

    Not as you promised to make me one. You didn't, and if I hoped you would I said nothing, because I was swept away, as you might call it. And anyway, Emily, you said, what difference would it make…?

James	What would it?
Emily	Look at all the unhappy marriages, you said…
James	Look at them.
Emily	Besides, you said, it's not the gold band. It's what you've seen and read and how you behave. Not, spider, that having seen and read and behaved I'm sure now that I wants to be that sort of lady…
James	Want.
Emily	Want. I likes the manners and the clothes, spider, and the hintellectual interests, but…
James	No h.
Emily	No h… But I don't like the lifting up of noses at those who don't have no aitches, and I always liked work, spider, even when it was gutting fish, and if you asks me all that makes most people ladies is money.
James	Ask.
Emily	Ask me.
James	Spider?
Emily	You didn't see him?
James	No.
Emily	That corner. At the end of a very long thread.

She flashes him again.

> Boo...!

Again no massive response.

> Sorry.

James You don't really want it, do you?

She considers.

Emily Too late, ain't it, wouldn't you say?

Does this mean now, or for ever?

> Troppo tarde.

James They do say your Italian grammar's better than your English.

Emily They?

James They.

Emily When you're off and about with they, James, do you know what I do?

He does not want to go there.

But she waits.

James You said that Maria arranged singing lessons.

Emily She did.

James With her – what d'you call it?

Emily In French? Répétiteur.

That's it. Yes. Répétiteur.

> I like your Maria. And she likes me. We like each other.

James Yes.

Emily Just as well. Can't scratch her eyes out, can I? Not if I'm half a lady, that is.

*James *gets up.*

But why?

He doesn't grab her.

He takes a deep draught from his flask.

She watches.

	What are you scared of? You can tell me. What?
James	I've got to find something that doesn't fail me. Or that I don't mess up.
Emily	You had nightmares again last night. Moans and shouts in your sleep. I tried to hold you but you woke up.
James	I don't remember.
Emily	You must know what some of them are.
James	I don't.

She does not believe him.

	I know that I've dreamed, but I don't know what about.
Emily	I used to dream that I'd have shoes.
James	When I saw you I thought: with her I can be what I want. I can achieve that great thing or other.
Emily	But now you can't.
James	Maybe I'm afraid of whatever it is.
Emily	Not much use, then, am I?
James	I love the way you hold your ground. Always did. Can't resist it.

He mechanically opens her gown and mechanically closes it.

He drinks and then consults his watch.

Emily   Late.

James   Yes.

Emily   You'd better go.

James   What about you?

Emily   I've got my lesson.

James   Lesson?

Emily   Singing.

James   Here?

Emily   At the Academy.

James   You can't walk there alone.

Emily   Littimer escorts me.

James   What's all this about, Emily?

Emily   All this?

James   What's it about?

Emily   Singing.

Don't exasperate me.

James   You're not pregnant, are you?

Emily   No.

James   No?

Emily   No.

James   But you'd like to be?

Emily   Showed me all the bedroom tricks, James, didn't you?

James   How not to get pregnant being one.

Emily	Besides, what sort of a father would you make, d'you reckon?
James	Not good.
Emily	No.

She studies him.

He very deliberately decides to have another drink at the moment.

	Yet there's plenty looked up to you, haven't they?
James	Well, I treat them all the same, don't I?
Emily	Davy Copperfield for one.
James	Little daisy David. I thought I'd miss him, but I can't say I do.
Emily	He's done what you haven't, though, James.
James	What's that?
Emily	Sat down and made money with his pen.
James	I don't need to make money.
Emily	You don't want to be a poet, then?
James	He's not a poet. He's a shorthand reporter in Parliament.
Emily	He wrote them sketches as well, didn't he? About that fat chap with spectacles.
James	Not them for God's sake. Those.
Emily	Sorry.
James	Don't keep saying sorry.
Emily	One day I won't be.
James	What?

Emily I'm bursting, James, like a child what needs bigger clothes.

James Not what.

Emily That. That. For which although I know you're a scoundrel I'm very grateful.

James starts to speak.

Checks himself.

Then his tone is different.

James We'll have better times again, Emily. Of course we will. I tell you what. Get dressed and come with me.

Emily My lesson, James. Can't miss it.

James Just this once…

Emily Sorry…

He wants to persist but decides not to.

James Well then. When I get back…

She smiles.

He picks up his light outdoor coat and hat.

So. How do I look? An English gentleman?

Emily Always.

He smiles.

Then after a moment he goes.

She's alone.

She takes a deep breath and rings the service handbell.

The manservant Littimer appears.

Littimer Has he gone?

Emily Help me…

She leads the way into the bedroom.

Scene Two   **Naples**   **1837**

The same. Some hours later. Lamp lit. Night. The room different somehow – something missing.

Steerforth arrives, a little the worse for wear.

James Emily?

No response.

      Emily? Littimer! Littimer!

Littimer *appears.*

      Oh. There you are.

Littimer Did you receive my message?

James Message?

Littimer At the theatre, sir.

James For God's sake. I was fucking Maria in the back of the carriage, how could I –

He stops. He senses the urgency.

      What?

Littimer She's gone, sir.

James Emily?

Littimer Gone, sir.

James *goes into the bedroom.*

Comes out again.

James Littimer, what the hell have you – Did you take her to the singing lesson?

Littimer Sir, I –

James Did you take her?

Littimer Yes.

James Did you wait?

Littimer Of course I –

James Did you wait?

Littimer *wants to explain but realises that* **James** *is not actually listening.*

James *swigs from his flask.*

Then he will listen but still blames **Littimer.**

　　　　　　For the third time. Did you wait?

Littimer She left by another door.

James Another door?

Littimer Sir, I never sit in the room during the lesson.

James Where do you sit?

Littimer In the corridor.

James Until she comes out?

Littimer Yes.

James How old's the teacher?

Littimer How old?

James Has she gone with him? Is it him?

Littimer He's an old man. White hair.

James	But he tricked you?
Littimer	Sir, I think that she left with his blessing.
James	His blessing? What the hell does that mean?
Littimer	He knew her intentions and approved of them.
James	Explain! What happened? Why?
Littimer	Sir, Miss Emily had a carriage bring her here, where I suspect that she had already packed her valise, and then went to the quay.
James	The quay?
Littimer	She took a boat, sir.
James	Where to?
Littimer	Palermo.
James	On her own? To Palermo. She's no money. How can she go to Palermo?
Littimer	Sir –
James	Does she know anybody in Palermo?
Littimer	Sir, she went with the opera, sir. She's one of the singers.

Steerforth stops. Something falls into place.

James My God.

He understands more.

> Do you mean the second company? The ones sent to fill out the chorus?

Littimer	Yes.
James	Did you know? Did she tell you?
Littimer	Me, sir? Why would she tell me, sir?

James stares. A bit of a drunken challenge.

Littimer holds his ground.

He did know, of course.

But **James** *sees beyond him.*

James It's Maria, isn't it? Schemed the whole biscuit barrel. Very Italian, Maria bloody lyric soprano Bertinotti who I'm fucking from here to Pompeii every afternoon. Flattered Emily along. Got rid of her at one swoop. How stupid can somebody - ? Didn't you realise what was happening?

Littimer Begging your pardon, sir, but didn't you?

James What?

More things fall into place.

Starts to speak.

Stops.

I hate this. Hate losing at cards. Hate losing people. I thought that young Emily had begun to grow up. I mean after those tantrums in Cologne...

Searching himself.

Where's my flask?

Littimer Might you look in your pocket, sir?

James Er. Yes. Right.

It is there.

You've been a good ally. Thank you.

Drinks.

> I know that after Cologne I said that Emily was a dead duck hanging round my neck so why don't I give you money so that you can marry her to make her respectable and then go back to Yarmouth or wherever it was and the chapel-goers ever after.

Gestures. Wherever. You know what I mean.

Littimer   I never did see myself in Yarmouth, sir.

James   No?

Littimer   No, sir.

James   But you could have set yourselves up. Public house. Carriage hire...

Maybe.

> But I couldn't do it, could I? I couldn't bring myself to throw Emily away. I threw that woman in Weymouth, didn't I, and I cried all the way back to London, but I couldn't... I mean there's something about Emily that... Did you resent my turnaround?

Littimer   Not at all, sir.

James   She could be a hell of a woman.

Littimer   It's not for me to comment, sir.

James   She can't really sing, can she?

Littimer   I believe them to have assured her that she can.

James   Good God.

Another thought strikes him.

> Who paid?

Littimer   Paid?

James	For the lessons.
Littimer	Didn't you?
James	No.
Littimer	Oh.
James	I can't believe Madonna Maria went that far, I mean, I thought… I don't know what I thought. I…

He gestures. Staggers. Finds himself sitting on the floor.

> Boredom, Littimer. Where's the use in anything. I'm bloody angry, though. How dare they?

Littimer Help you up, sir?

He holds out his hand.

James *takes it.*

James Pack. Everything. What's left of hers as well. We'll go.

Littimer *holds him up.*

Littimer Where to, sir? Home? White cliffs of Dover, sir?

James Palermo.

Littimer Palermo?

James Of course. Palermo. Where else?

They go into the bedroom to pack.

Scene Three   **Rome**   **1839**

Henri *and* **Emily** *stroll in the Borghese gardens.*

Henri   That we meet again is, as you say, a coincidence. But in life, Madame Emilia, there are many more coincidences than in romantic fiction. It is for us to seize their importance…

Emily   That may very well be the case, but if you seize my bum again I'll make a scene.

Henri   Here?

Emily   Here.

Henri   In the Borghese Gardens?

Emily   In the Borghese Gardens.

Henri   Shall we sit on this… the wood?

Emily   Bench.

Henri   Bench of convenience?

Emily   Convenient bench.

Henri   As you say.

They sit.

               I am, it sequences, besotted by you.

Emily   Oh, Henri. Rubbish. You just want me to be besotted by you.

Henri   You perceive?

Emily   You have this daft idea that you need to fascinate every woman you meet.

Henri	Not at all. How can I? I'm very ugly.
Emily	You are.

He gestures. So there it is.

He is also a bit put out.

	I didn't mean that.
Henri	No.
Emily	But you must know what I do mean.
Henri	I hope…

They ponder it.

	Feelings arise. I behave this way or that. People don't know what I am.
Emily	I know what you are.

He looks.

	You're a ridiculously marvelous little feller.
Henri	Feller?
Emily	Chap. Man. Bloke.
Henri	Bloke…

They ponder this.

	But we have strolled here, I think, for you to offer me the exposition of the coincidence.
Emily	How come I can talk to you as easy as easy?
Henri	I'm French.
Emily	Is that it?

He gestures: isn't it?

She considers. Maybe it is.

> My Italian's good now. Had you noticed?

Henri The exposition…

Emily Actually, I don't know what exposition means.

He lets this pass.

Henri How many years ago we meet in Bologna?

Shrugs. Four? Five?

> You are the inamorata of milord Steerforth…

Emily He's not a milord.

Henri The girl he has seduced.

Emily Yes.

Henri Then depuis how many years later I see the opera in Rome and you are the diva. Emilia Peggotta. And my God but you are good. And I can say this, because I heard Malibran, and Pasta, and Caroline Ungher.

Emily Ungher?

Henri The one who sang the soprano in Beethoven's Ninth Symphony, and at the end she turns him, to see the applause he cannot hear…

They ponder this for a moment.

> In Palermo you were in the chorus. Then the soprano loses her voice and you are called upon. Bravo. A triumph. Victory. The musical Austerlitz. This I comprehend.

Emily She was lucky.

Henri Little Peggotty?

Scene Three

Emily To become La Peggotta.

Henri This is what Napoleon said. Give me a general who has luck.

Emily Very true.

Henri But then what happens? La Peggotta becomes the donna fatale. The sensation who has lovers. Seven, they gossip in the cafes.

Emily Actually it's five.

Henri Three marchesi, they say, and four -

Emily No, no. And a poet, and a music critic.

Henri A critic?

Emily To write me up.

Henri Of course.

Emily And the worse the gossip the more it sells seats.

Henri Yes...

They think about it.

Then he begins to come to the point.

And where in this histoire, if I may ask, is milord Steerforth?

Emily Nowhere, so far as I know.

Henri That is, in your affections?

Emily I left him. Ran off. Had to.

They think about it.

I still like him. Sort of . If I ever think about him.

Henri But he does not like himself.

Sharp, **Henri**. *Very sharp.*

Emily	No.
Henri	Why not?
Emily	He's not a milord.
Henri	Not a milord? Ridiculous. In the world, how many are born milords?
Emily	What was your father?
Henri	A lawyer.
Emily	Steerforth's was in trade.
Henri	All the English are in trade. Even milords who pretend not to be.
Emily	Sugar.
Henri	Sugar?
Emily	Plantations. Money from slaves.

He starts to speak.

Stops.

Thinks.

Henri	You remember that I say I wish to confess to you?
Emily	You did confess. You're besotted.
Henri	Of course. But not that.
Emily	I said phooey and don't you touch my bum.
Henri	Loving you was politeness, Emilia. What I confess is that I saw him.
Emily	Him?
Henri	Milord Steerforth.
Emily	James? Where?

Henri	Here.
Emily	In Rome?
Henri	Yes.
Emily	When?
Henri	This morning.
Emily	What?

Takes it in.

> Where?

Henri	In the café.
Emily	Was he drunk?

Not the question he expected.

> You're not sure?

Henri	No.
Emily	What did he say?
Henri	We did not speak.
Emily	Did he see you?
Henri	I was about to enter. I dot him.
Emily	Spot.
Henri	Spot him. I turn away.
Emily	Why?
Henri	I have sent my note to the theatre. You have replied. We are to meet, after a long time. Gossip says that you and the milord are apart, but I am not sure. I decided to be discreet.
Emily	Thank you…

Henri Does he know that La Peggotta is you?

Emily He must. Mustn't he?

Henri But you have not seen him?

Emily Since I slipped away? No.

Henri Gossip says that he looks for you.

Emily Yes.

They consider this.

Then he sees something.

Henri My God, what did we say, about coincidence?

She looks.

Emily Oh, no!

Henri Alas, yes. It is our friend milord Steerforth, who falls out of the carriage and comes towards us with his stick…

James *is there, followed by* **Littimer**.

James You damned blockhead, Henri, French-kiss slobbering over every woman you meet. Was it you? Did you take her away from me, you swine?

He swings at **Henri** *with his stick, but overbalances, and but for* **Littimer** *catching him would fall over.*

Where is he? Never trust a frog-eater. Bloody Bonaparte. Why didn't you leave a note?

Emily What more could it have said?

James You do realise that it's taken me two years to find you?

Emily Then you're not a very good looker, are you?

James	Was it our fault that the boat we took to Palermo was blown by a storm to Sardinia?
Emily	You look terrible. You're bloated. Do you realize? Do you care?
James	And what's more, we've carted your clothes all over Italy.
Emily	You've what?
James	You left half your clothes behind.
Emily	Because they reminded me of who I used to be.
James	You don't care about them. My God. I suddenly feel very dizzy.

He sits down.

	Littimer can explain the rest.
Emily	What?
Littimer	Begging your pardon, Miss – Madame Emilia, but the fact is that we cut them to pieces with knives.
Emily	My clothes?
James	I did half an hour a week of it, for a month or two.
Littimer	It assuaged sir's feelings, as you might say.
Emily	You cut up my clothes?
James	Oh, don't worry. We kept all the shreds. I was going to stick them up your what not.

Emily *starts to protest but* **Henri**'s *gesture halts her.*

Henri	Mes amis, might I not act as the examining magistrate?
James	Ever the diplomat, eh, Henri? Ever the facilitating bureaucrat.

Henri	I had that training as you know, my dear old James, in the days of the Empire.
James	Waterloo. Up guards and at 'em. St Helena, and I don't mean a variety of lavender.
Henri	This is humour of poor taste, don't you think, Emilia?
Emily	I do, and in my opinion it's to cover embarrassment.
Henri	And the disconcertion, I should say.
James	Disconcertion?
Henri	This is not a word?
James	Is it?
Littimer	Search me, sir.
Emily	Well whether it's a word or not, it's a blank look like the one on your face.
Henri	And I know what it means, James, and so I think do you. Your rage has evaporate. No?
James	Evaporated.
Henri	Evaporated. You are face to face with Emilia and to your surprise what do you feel?
James	Not much.
Henri	Not much.
Emily	Not much?
James	Well, what do you feel?

She seems about to reel off a catalogue.

But she doesn't.

But, again, she must have a final word.

Emily	I just wish you'd pay proper attention to your health.
James	I take cold water plunges whenever I can.
Emily	Apart from that I don't feel anything.
Henri	Survive our own feelings or die, says the magistrate.
James	Very true.
Emily	Bloody annoying, actually.

Littimer *makes a face.*

	What's the matter with you?
James	He hates to hear a lady swear.
Emily	I'm not a lady. I'm a diva. Cross my heart and fiddle de di.
Littimer	Beg pardon, madam.
Emily	Eau de vie and the bella figura. So what's next?
James	Er…

They look from one to the other.

It is clearly **Henri**, *they realise, who will have the answer.*

Henri	Thank you. Might we not, milord Steerforth, take your carriage to the café, and after a libation go our separate ways? Characters, as it were, in some fable.
Emily	We might, actually, oh master of the diplomatic arts.
James	Do you know, I felt I can't think how many times in my life that I was on the edge of being what I could be, but never so strongly as I do at this instant…

He stands and offers his arm.

	Will you accept my arm, miss diva?
Emily	As a compliment, or to stop you falling over?
James	Whichever you please. How merry it is to be civilized. Shall we?

She takes his arm.

Off they go to the carriage.

Scene Four   Fiesole   1840

The terrace of a villa. **Littimer** *comes out in response to what he has seen from the window.*

David *arrives. It has been a bit of a climb up the hill.*

The view of Florence is of course breathtaking.

Littimer	Mr Copperfield, sir? In Italy? My word.
David	You're a rogue, Littimer. Always were and always will be. Where's James Steerforth?

Littimer *raises a temporising hand.*

	Don't raise your hand to me, man. Where is he?
Littimer	He's dressing sir. Will you wait here on the terrace?
David	Where's Emily? Is she with him? Or has he thrown her away already?
Littimer	Sir, I er…
David	You may as well know that…
Littimer	…must tell you that…

Scene Four

David My mission in Italy has been and is to rescue her, and whatever may have happened to her reputation, to restore her to her rightful, loving and forgiving family. So. Where is she?

Littimer *is doing his best to be discreet.*

Littimer Sir, please be restrained until I can announce your arrival.

David Have you no sense of the damage you've done?

Littimer I am the man, sir. Not the master.

David You're the blackguard who smuggled her out of Yarmouth.

Littimer She was very willing contraband.

David What?

Littimer I apologise for answering back, sir. But please. Be aware. What you will see in Mr James is a great change. And I shall shortly be leaving him.

David Leaving him?

Littimer He no longer needs me.

David Why not?

Littimer As I say, sir. I am working out my notice.

David What d'you mean? A change? What's happened? Is he ill? Where is Emily?

Again **Littimer** *puts out his hands to appeal for patience.*

David *takes matters into his own, and shouts.*

Emily! Emily! Come out of the house! I'm here! All's well again!

Littimer	Madame – Miss Emily is not with us here in Fiesole, sir, and never has been.
David	You're lying. Not here? Where is she?
Littimer	When last we heard, she was in Bologna.
David	Bologna? Why? Where is Bologna? I'll go there at once. After all, why waste my time on James Steerforth?

Steerforth is there. He is dressed as a woman.

James	Oh. Oh dear, Daisy. I'm sorry to hear you say that.
David	Forgive me, signora. We have not had the pleasure, and when this man gives me instructions as regards Bologna I must -

He stops.

Amazed.

Shocked.

	James?
James	Jemima.
David	Jemima?
James	Well. It's clear that, for example, the feminine of Victor is Victoria, but we weren't positive about James, so I plumped for Jemima.
David	You're engaged in theatricals, you mean? Charades? Some sort of – Littimer. Is the change you indicated that Mr Steerforth has lost his reason?
James	Harry, with his theological qualifications, and his interest in the early Celtic saints, pointed out that in various Gaelics James is Seamus and Sean, and

there are of course Shaunas and Sheenas, and Shauna Steerforth does have a sort of music hall ring to it, wouldn't you say, but – Sit down, Daisy, old thing, you look very disconcerted.

David   Thank you...

James   Do you struggle for breath?

David   The climb up the hill.

James   Of course.

Littimer   Might I suggest cordials, gentlemen, and a hard biscuit?

James   I think so, Littimer. Well done.

Littimer *goes inside.*

David *tries to collect himself.*

You look older than you did, Daisy, but every bit as innocent.

David   For heaven's sake, you –

He checks himself.

He's still not entirely sure that he isn't dealing with a madman.

James   As I was saying. Shauna, not to mention Sheena, seemed lower-class, somehow, if not a little too racy...

David   Too racy?

James   ... whereas Jemima is more blissfully domestic. It's more connubial, as when Harry pats my hand and says "Jemima, my dear, don't worry your pretty head about that."

David   That?

James	That.
David	What d'you mean: that? What is that?
James	That is whatever, at the time, men are getting into a froth about.
David	Men.
James	Men, Daisy. The great frothers.
David	James – Jemima – Might I ask you? Who is this Henry of whom you speak? Does he, I mean, well…
James	Does he what?
David	Does he truly exist?
James	As large as life. He's my husband.

David *tries to speak.*

Can't.

Then he can.

David	You mean: you believe yourself to be married?
James	Harry did send a boy up the hill to tell us you were coming. I don't suppose Littimer mentioned it.
David	I – No. – I – what he did say is that he's leaving your service.
James	Yes. Well. I need a lady's maid, don't I?
David	James – Jemima – You surely don't go out into the streets in these clothes?
James	I'm growing my hair long. What do you think?
David	Your hair was always a sort of golden and heroic banner, I suppose, I – I mean I…

James	Don't blush. But I'll still take it as a compliment.
David	How did – Forgive me, but this is – How did Harry *know* that I was seeking you?
James	You asked him, so he told you where we were.
David	What?
James	I'd described everything about you before, of course, and about Emilia and jolly old Henri Beyle. Well, Harry knew Henri, of course (Harry and Henri. Quite comical, eh?) and he even knew Henri's books, as I suppose he would. Then, my word, but if Henri himself didn't write us a letter. He'd met you, he said. Some trouble with luggage, he said.
David	You mean – Henri is the Frenchman at the Customs Post?
James	You give them twenty scudi. That's all it takes.
David	Yes. So your French friend – My God.
James	What?
David	*(Realising who he might be)* Harry…
James	He potted up all those geraniums. Green fingers. Won't leave it to the garden boys. Ah! Ecco! The cordials!

Littimer *is in with the tray.*

Sets it down.

Pours.

David *starts to speak.*

Stops.

Starts again.

Stops.

James　　You dip the biscuits in the wine. Do you know?

David　　Yes.

Dips.

Nibbles.

It's crumbly and catches in his throat.

They move to help.

I'm fine, he gestures.

He drinks.

It's pungent.

Gasps.

Coughs.

Can speak.

David　　Harry isn't by any chance the Reverend Henry Molyneux Molyneux –Smithson, is he?

James　　He is. D.D. M.A. Oxon. Fellow of the Society of Antiquaries.

David　　The curate of the English church in Florence.

James　　The very same. Down the hill.

David　　My God…

He drinks his drink.

Littimer *pours another.*

David *drains that.*

Then whispers.

David　　Do people know?

James	*(whispering back)* Who cares?
David	*(whisper)* But what do you <u>do</u>?
James	*(whisper)* Buggery. Like we all did at school. You surely remember.

David *gets up.*

Paces.

Clears his throat.

Speaks.

David	What I must ask you, James – Jemima – James, what I must insist upon – My responsibility, that is – Emily. Where is she, and what happened?
James	Excellent question. What did happen, Littimer? What did?
David	Can't you tell me yourself? Why ask him?
Littimer	It is very often the case, Mr Copperfield, sir, that the servant sees more than the master.
David	Just tell me what happened.
Littimer	Mr James, sir, was a man who wanted to be moved by deep feelings, but never was.
James	Deep fears, Daisy. That's what I had. Surely you above all realise that?
Littimer	Mr James was soon bored, Mr Copperfield, and he was very soon bored by Miss Emily, who screamed and shouted at first, but then as she saw more of the world – Well, the fact is that she blossomed, sir.
James	She did. She became a sort of deceptive whatever it is.
David	Whatever it is?

Littimer	To cut a long story short, sir, Mr James gave her money to have clothes made, but she spent it on singing lessons.
David	Singing?
James	Didn't old Henri tell you about the opera?
David	What he said was that – what?
James	Very discreet, isn't he? Doesn't call himself by other names for nothing.
David	Other names?
Littimer	De plume, sir.
David	What are you talking about?
James	He's a man of many worlds, Daisy.
David	I thought he was ridiculous.
James	That too. But he didn't mention Jemima, did he, and he didn't name La Peggotta.
David	Who's La Peggotta?
James	Emilia Peggotta. She's very famous in Italian opera.
David	You mean…
James	Yes.
David	La Peggotta?
James	Screeching. Melodrama. Very unreal. Old Henri loves it.
David	But how can a herring girl be an opera singer?
James	The only bit I like is the way the audience ignore the stage, and gossip. But then I'm an Englishman, aren't I?

David Come to that, how can any woman earn her own living and be respectable? I mean, does the Reverend Harry let his wife go out to work?

A second's contemplation.

Then –

James What I have been vouchsafed, Daisy – which is one of Harry's scriptual words. Vouchsafed. It sounds like a horse that won the Derby, doesn't it? What I have been vouchsafed is a vision of the future. We women won't be stopped, Daisy. Our instincts may be all over the place but they're still stronger than your ideas. We have far more whirligig energy.

David *starts to speak.*

Stops.

Drains his glass.

Sets it down.

Littimer *refills.*

Women won't be beaten, Daisy. So I decided to join them. I mean, look at Harry. How he wrestles with his sermons. Poor boy. All those ideas colliding in his brain. But he forgets them when I hold him in my arms.

David *drains his glass.*

Tries to stand.

Sits down.

David   I think I've had too many cordials quoo tickly.

They look at him.

Too quickly.

James   Don't worry. He needs something to line his stomach. Wouldn't you say?

Littimer   I would, sir.

James   The instant we heard you were coming we had the cook lay out the antipasti. Shall we go arm in arm…

David   My God…

Deep breath.

Up.

Arm in arm into the villa.

Littimer *follows with the tray.*

Epilogue   Pietra Sante   1840

Henri *is once again in the Tuscan customs post. And again reading.*

David *enters. This time he has bribed the officers.*

David   As fast as you can. Thank you . Grazie.

Stops.

Mutual recognition.

Monsieur Beyle?

Henri   Milord Copperfield?

David   I do declare.

Henri	The power of coincidence, to which I always refer.
David	You go South?
Henri	South. To my post in Civitavecchia. You?
David	North.
Henri	England?
David	England.

Henri *weighs it.*

Then –

Henri	So. I think you found your wandering Steerforth.
David	Yes.
Henri	And the young lady?
David	After a fashion.

Henri *waits.*

	I never managed to meet her, if that's what you mean.
Henri	Oh.
David	I did, however, discover that you and she and Steerforth are well acquainted.
Henri	Then you will understand why at our first meeting I was discreet.
David	Yes.
Henri	It was not for me to gossip.
David	No.
Henri	It was for you to discover.

David   Yes.

So that bit of honour is satisfied.

I did find James and – That is to say –

Henri   Yes.

David   It was from James and Jemima – I was told where Emily was, and I went there and tried to see her. I left my card at the stage door but there was no response. I discovered next day that she had left for an engagement elsewhere. I could, no doubt, have been more diligent. But in all the circumstances I decided not to follow. Jemima said that so far as he knew Emily had already sent a deal of money to her family in England.

Henri *absorbs this.*

Silence. They ponder.

A woman traveller comes in.

She wears a dust veil.

She takes it off to shake out.

*She is **Emilia**.*

*With huge joy she recognises **Henri**.*

He warns her.

Hush!

See who this is?

*She recognises **David**.*

She resumes her veil.

*This movement makes **David** aware of her.*

David   Signora.

She acknowledges.

Henri *invites her to sit.*

He knows what to do.

Henri   Did your Italian improve, Monsieur Copperfield?

David   Alas, no. Ordering in restaurants. That's about it.

Henri   Then you will excuse me if I converse with the lady?

David   Of course. Of course I will.

Henri   Thank you .

He turns to **Emily**.

    Do you want him to know who you are?

Emily   I don't think so.

Henri   You go to Milan?

Emily   Yes.

Henri   La Scala?

Emily   A Rossini.

Henri   I saw him two weeks ago in Paris. He asked about you.

Emily   Really?

Henri   She's northern, he said. North Europe. How does she compare with Caroline Ungher? More lyrical, I said. More feminine.

Emily   Thank you. Do northerners excite him?

Henri   His curiosity. Something different.

In their silence **David** *can speak in english.*

David	The fact is that Jemima – that James told me a lot about you.
Henri	He did?
David	An officer in the Grande Armée, he said.
Henri	Yes.
David	You met Napoleon.
Henri	Yes.
David	And you were on the retreat from Moscow…
Henri	I was.
David	What was it like?
Henri	It was cold.
David	Right…

Silence.

Emily	He does not even begin to recognise me.
Henri	Why would he? In his memory you are a fisher girl on the beach.

True, she supposes.

Meanwhile…

Emily	Did you see your doctor in Paris?
Henri	Geneva.
Emily	But you're well?
Henri	Well enough.
Emily	That means you aren't.
Henri	You really won't tell him who you are?
Emily	I never was the person he imagined.

Henri Never the innocent.

Emily No. Why rob him of that? Are you well or not?

He won't answer.

*She would force it but realises that to raise the emotional tempo might attract **David's** keener attention.*

*In the silence **David** can speak again.*

David James said that you're a wonderful writer. For English magazines, too. Under various pen-names, he said.

Henri *shrugs. Well, sometimes one's name <u>is</u> different.*

Your novel came out, did I hear?

Henri I hope you did.

David What's it called?

Henri The Charterhouse of Parma.

David Happy with it?

Henri Not so much with the publisher.

David Why not?

Henri He made me hack the end about, to fit two volumes.

David You didn't resist?

Henri I was tired.

Emily *reacts but stops herself.*

It means, she realises, that he is truly not well.

David Even so you're the person to whom I can confide my dilemma.

Henri What?

Emily I'm sorry. I interrupted.

David *does not understand her Italian.*

I excuse myself. Please.

Carry on, she means.

David Thank you. That is. Yes –

Henri Your dilemma?

David Emily and Jemima. What should I tell people in England?

Henri Have you considered the truth?

David Impossible.

Emily *reacts but covers it.*

Coughing.

David My goodness...

Henri My dear lady...

She waves away their solicitations.

David How can I tell England about Jemima? It's shocking. It's unnatural. Respectable English tourists visit Florence, and Jemima's so-called husband the curate welcomes and advises them. He orders stocks of leaf tea to entertain them.

Henri And Emilia?

David Can a woman work and still be respectable?

Emily Of course she can.

David What?

Emily Excuse me.

David	Surely, seduction must ruin a girl. So must there not be a cleansing? Repentance? Redemption? How can an idle and promiscuous life with a scoundrel be seen as educational?
Emily	Why doesn't one of us kick him in the balls?
Henri	Respectability, Emilia, is the new English battle-fleet.
Emily	I was born below decks. I couldn't afford it.
Henri	And now you can afford to ignore it.

To **David**.

	I met General the Marquis de Lafayette, you know. He would always look down the front of girls' dresses.
David	What?
Henri	And being old and a little deaf, he boomed. But exquisite politesse, you know.
David	Does that excuse him?
Henri	A hero of two revolutions who nevertheless looks down women's dresses? I don't know. But surely life is ambiguous.
David	My story must be simpler.
Henri	Simpler? More moral? Or more melodrama?
David	Both.
Emily	Oh my God…!
Henri	Very well. Might I suggest?
David	Please.

Henri	Milord Steerforth and Emilia quarrel. He abandons her. She is crazed.
David	Driven to despair?
Henri	Despair or the lascivious manservant. But she runs away.
David	Good.
Emily	Ridiculous.
David	Where?
Henri	To a life of prostitution.
David	Excellent.
Emily	Sentimental bollocks.
Henri	Not, alas, to the English reader.
David	Is she redeemed?
Henri	Of course: eventually.
David	Found. Forgiven. Taken home.
Henri	Perfect.
Emily	Boring.
Henri	And Jemima?
David	You mean James.
Henri	James.
David	James, weary of debauchery, returns to England in despair, and… And what…?
Emily	Shipwreck.
Henri	Shipwreck.
David	Shipwreck. In the greatest storm ever seen, James is drowned, his ship destroyed upon the very shore

where Emily the woman he corrupted has gambolled as a child of innocence...

They survey the edifice they have created.

Henri   Immortal...

Emily   Incredible.

David   I hope you mean that...

Henri   But you, milord David.

David   Me?

Henri   Where, in this narrative, do you place yourself?

David   Oh. Er – Yes. Sadder. Wiser. But, somehow, without blame.

Henri   Perfect.

Emily   My arse.

David   Thank you.

David *is so relieved that he does not see* **Littimer** *at the door.*

Henri   And here, madame, is your manservant.

Littimer *sees* **David**.

Emily *warns* **Littimer**.

Littimer *floats away.*

Henri *marvels at the narrow escape.*

              Your carriage.

Emily   Yes.

Henri   Write to me.

Emily   I will.

Henri   Good journey.

Emily *acknowledges* **David**.

Emily   Signor.

David   Oh. Yes. Er. Signora.

David *does, perhaps, glimpse* **Littimer** *as they leave.*

> Charming woman. Most assured. Continental, of course.

A thought does strike him.

Was it?

It can't have been.

> What I particularly like about our concoction is the shipwreck. I mean, I can see old Jemima being heroic in a shipwreck, and while we're at it why can't Littimer drown with him? I mean –

The thought persists.

He goes to the door.

Looks back and forth.

Was it or wasn't it?

> My word. But I could have sworn for a moment that –

But it can't have been.

Can it?

Henri   Has the lady's carriage gone?

David   Yes.

Henri   Are they ready with yours?

David   What? Oh. Yes. I think they are.

Time to go.

Shake hands.

        Thank you. Once again. Thank you.

Henri   Safe journey.

David   And yourself. Retreat from Moscow. Italy. For better or worse, eh?

He hesitates for an instant.

Then goes.

Henri *is alone.*

Looks.

Thinks.

Is amused.

Then as he, too, goes, he hears the opera in his head.

The End

St Boniface Gardens

CHARACTERS

Karl Marx   a German born writer and agitator, aged 63

James Williamson   a General Practitioner, aged 34

Eleanor Marx   nicknamed Tussy, Marx's daughter, aged 26

Mrs Williamson   the doctor's wife, probably in her late 20s

SETTING

Marx rented rooms from the landlady Miss Maclaren at 1 St Boniface Gardens, Ventnor, on the Isle of Wight, and there, and outside Dr Williamson's house, is where the action takes place, between November 1882 and March 1883.

MUSIC

Piano music should provide an Overture and take us through each scene break.

See Stage Direction between Scene Six and the Epilogue.

Ideally this music would be played live.

Scene One   The Sitting Room   Morning   November 7, 1882

*Empty. Knocking at the door. Then **Marx** comes in from the bedroom, scrambling into a dressing-gown over trousers and combinations. He has been up, half-dressed, and dozed again.*

Marx   Yes. Wait. What is the time? Wait. I can't find – Yes, I hear. Come in.

***Dr James Williamson** is 34 years old. He was born in South Shields. He has wide interests and is wise beyond his years.*

Williamson   Doctor Marx?

Marx   What is the time?

Williamson   Nine fifteen. Did you fall asleep again?

Marx   Who are you? Are you Doctor Williamson?

Williamson   Yes.

Marx   I am most thankful to see you. Allow me to explain. What always occurs here is that –

Coughing and difficult breath overtake him.

Williamson   Might we sit down?

Marx   Please. To explain, I –

But it is easier to sit and recover than to explain.

Williamson *seeks first to give him time.*

Williamson   When Miss Maclaren called me she said that you experienced some sort of relapse during the night.

Marx   In the mind. My sickness comes always from the mind.

Williamson You've had news that distressed you?

Marx Not this time. Not news, but continual worries. Did Miss Maclaren explain about my daughters?

Williamson I have known Miss Maclaren for some years, and like any sympathetic letter of rooms she is discreet about her guests. A virtue, don't you agree, in what is, after all, a health resort?

Marx is both pleased and amused by this.

Marx Well said. Good. I do agree. She was very understanding when my youngest daughter became upset. At my concern for her older sister, a most difficult – It was on our previous visit.

Williamson Which was earlier this year, she said. And you stayed here for about a month?

Marx My wife had died. My health was poor. New scenery, we thought, might help our grief. But it rained and my daughter was agitated. We returned to London.

Williamson So this present time you came alone.

Marx The last day of October.

Williamson Since when we've had a week of heavy rain, for which I apologise. It's usually more kind. But until last night you'd seemed very well, Miss Maclaren says.

Marx I was: and with patience and self-control I am convinced that I will soon be once again in shape and able to work.

Scene One 177

Williamson	I hope you will. So what has happened?
Marx	I have deep fears that come to me in dreams.
Williamson	Last night?
Marx	I see violence and deaths. I am to blame. Flames within forests. People with no faces but I know who they are. I am in terror. I wake up. Gasp. Cough. All my old pains.

Williamson *thinks for a second and is then specific.*

Williamson	Which are respiratory?
Marx	Respiratory.
Williamson	Do you think, Doctor Marx, that before I examine you, you could give me some brief notion of your medical history?
Marx	I respect that. Proceed by logic. I see why you are recommended.
Williamson	Where should you start, do you think?
Marx	Where would you?
Williamson	At the beginning?
Marx	I was a most healthy child.
Williamson	Which bodes well. So that old scar on your face – a fall?
Marx	A duel.
Williamson	You don't say.
Marx	I was a very wild German student, you know, and I drank like a huge fish and –

Stops. Sees himself as he was, perhaps.

How can he explain all this to so young an Englishman?

	Might I ask – What do you know about me?
Williamson	Not much. That you're a political philosopher.

You could call it that.

	And regarded by many, perhaps, as extreme.
Marx	I fear so.

Time to move on.

Williamson	Was the duel a matter of honour?
Marx	A fraternity ritual.
Williamson	Of course.
Marx	Crazy, you know. The ludicrousness of a ruling class.
Williamson	Which, from what little I've been told, I understand to be the very thing that you have rejected.
Marx	This is your dry sense of humour is it not?
Williamson	Probably.
Marx	Myself I am more for the jokes about trouser-splitting.
Williamson	To what extent, would you say, have your health problems been due to the circumstances of your life?

Scene One 179

*This stops **Marx** short for an instant.*

But he likes this young man.

Marx Good. I like this. The direct engagement. Well. I have always, you know, been my own chief medical counsel. Always. When I was a student I wanted to be a poet and I had a mental breakdown because my poems were no good. I was a failure. I resolved it by long walks and the study of philosophy. Which took me to history, and how we might understand and improve the world, but nobody pays wages for such speculations, you know. And when study is allied to political activity we become a danger, and are persecuted. So. Well. Then I married. Children. No money. Scraps of journalism. And as a person unable, somehow, to control the functions of my energy, I was sometimes idle with no inspiration, and sometimes I would work, work, work. Hours at a stretch. Darkness to dawn. Rum and cigars to oil the machine but never able to afford decent Havanas, you know, always cheap – Well –

Williamson Do you still smoke?

Not so much.

Starts to explain.

Coughs.

Williamson Cheap cigars made you ill?

Marx Anger, young man. It was anger that ravaged me. Always anger at the world and at shallow, stupid, cruel people. Frustrated. How could my energies burst the dam? They could not. It was a constipation, of society itself immovable inside me.

Williamson There was actual pain?

Marx Headaches. Rheumatism. Toothache. Doctors hummed. Doctors hawed. I prescribed myself arsenic as the anaesthetic. While writing, you know, while struggling to solve the most mighty problems. And my wife endured the consequences. She was a baroness, you know, not the landed but the bureaucratic nobility, but of great refinement still. Having been thrown out of Europe we lived in two rooms in your London Soho. She was pregnant seven times. Three survive. My struggle was the reef upon which her life was wrecked.

He stops. Realising perhaps that he has said more than he intended.

But he must go on.

Then I was plagued by boils.

Williamson Boils?

Marx The outbursts of my rage. Inside my thigh. On my arse. My shoulder blade. One at the very junction of the body and the penis, the inconvenience of which I am sure you can imagine.

Scene One 181

Williamson	I can.
Marx	I have never before spoken to a doctor with such frankness.
Williamson	I've forgotten to ask how old you are.
Marx	Sixty-three.
Williamson	Have your boils persisted?
Marx	I would lance them with an open razor.
Williamson	If you are ever tempted to do that again, please cleanse the blade first in a flame.
Marx	No need. They have left me.
Williamson	How come?
Marx	Immersion in sea water, and both mineral and Turkish baths.
Williamson	Any other self-cures?
Marx	I once almost choked myself on raspberry vinegar.
Williamson	Goodness me.
Marx	Whenever I catch cold, and catarrh and bronchitis ensue, I anoint my neck and chest with iodine.

Well, **Williamson** *seems to say, that is a bit more sensible.*

Williamson	But at the same time - forgive me – at the same time your material circumstances would seem to have improved.
Marx	My friend and colleague Mr Engels sold his business in Manchester, which enabled him to retire to London, and to

	provide me with a small but more or less sufficient annuity. Our circumstances became more suited to my wife's dignity.
Williamson	With corresponding improvements to your health?
Marx	Yes. And then, most ludicrously, I was diagnosed as having an elongated liver.
Williamson	How was that treated?
Marx	We took the waters at Carlsbad.
Williamson	Really?
Marx	Two or three times.
Williamson	Fascinating.
Marx	It is.
Williamson	What was the regime, exactly?
Marx	At six a.m. one drinks the first two glasses of the waters. Then walking up and down for fifteen minutes. Then two glasses. Then walk for fifteen minutes. Then two glasses. Then walk for an hour.
Williamson	By which time it's what? About eight?
Marx	Eight and a coffee. After which the day is one's own. Conversations with amusing old ladies. Little orchestras. Etcetera. Another cold glass of the waters in the evening. Early to bed.
Williamson	Is the flavour of the waters distinctive?
Marx	Very. A simultaneous staleness and invigoration.

Scene One   183

Williamson	And you were helped?
Marx	Ameliorated: but it became impossible to return.
Williamson	Why was that?
Williamson	The German government passed laws against Socialism. I could have been arrested in transit.
Williamson	Oh.
Marx	Indeed. And as a reaction I collapsed. I was forbidden any activity, even reading the newspapers, because of their effect upon my temper.
Williamson	So what did you do?
Marx	We came to the Isle of Wight.
Williamson	When?
Marx	Eighteen Seventy Four.
Williamson	To Ventnor?
Marx	Ryde.
Williamson	It did you good?
Marx	Very much so. I took up all the island newspapers, which are amusing as you know, and visited the library in the Sandown Public Bath House. We walked and enjoyed the excursion steamer, from which we first saw Ventnor. We would have stayed longer, but a grandson died and we –

Stops.

In churning thoughts again.

> My anger now is caused by the fact that my two elder daughters are married to unpalatable men. It is a most disappointing and –

He stops himself.

Williamson *waits.*

> A year later, in Eighteen Seventy Five, my late wife and a friend visited Shanklin.

More thoughts.

Again **Williamson** *waits.*

Marx	Strange.
Williamson	What?
Marx	I had thought that memories of my wife would agitate me, and my coughing return. But I am calm.
Williamson	Which is the time to examine you, if I may.
Marx	Of course.
Williamson	Is that a vest or the top half of combinations?
Marx	Combinations.
Williamson	You couldn't wriggle out of it, could you?

Marx *can, after slipping down his gown. But awkwardly.*

So that he stops.

Marx Wriggle when young. When old, struggle.

Mutual smiles.

Then job done.

Williamson Thank you.

Williamson *has his stethoscope at the ready.*

Breathe in. And exhale. And again. Thank you. Again.

Then he taps and listens.

Once, twice more.

Then breaths again.

Another breath if you could. Thank you. And exhale.

Marx *wheezes a bit.*

It was more of an effort than he hoped.

Thank you. Very good.

Williamson *indicates: you can dress again.*

He puts away his stethoscope, and fishes out a medicine. He is conversational.

Where else have you taken health cures? Anywhere interesting?

Marx Indeed. After the death of my wife and our first stay in Ventnor my unmarried daughter Eleanor and I – she chain smokes, you know, and experiences insomnia and headaches and biliousness even though she refuses to eat. We were

	very unhappy. We went to – Well, Italy was out of the question, of course.
Williamson	Oh?
Marx	Only months ago a man was arrested there simply for his name.
Williamson	His name?
Marx	Marx.
Williamson	My goodness.
Marx	Indeed. So we went to Algiers.
Williamson	Exotic?
Marx	I was too numb to savour it. I seldom read the newspapers, even. I sat in the botanical gardens. Looking at the sea. And for some reason I had my hair and beard cut.
Williamson	Some reason?
Marx	I was no longer myself, I suppose.
Williamson	Oh.
Marx	Then Monte Carlo. Then to see my daughter Jennychen in France. Then Switzerland. Vevey.
Williamson	Picturesque?
Marx	I would have lived in Switzerland, you know. All the socialists are there and it is cheaper than London. But.
Williamson	What?
Marx	But there is no British Museum Reading Room.

Williamson	No. So. Now. You told Miss Maclaren, she said, that you were last examined in London three weeks ago and that since then your cough has diminished.
Marx	Yes.
Williamson	I would have thought as much. Good. I'll leave you with this liniment for exterior application, and call again in a couple of days. In the meantime no outdoors.
Marx	No?
Williamson	No. House arrest until I release you.
Marx	House arrest.
Williamson	It's better than prison, I'm sure.
Marx	Having been in some, I can assure you that it is.
Williamson	Jolly good.

Bag snapped shut. Ready.

Marx I will see you to the door, young man, and thank Miss Maclaren.

They go.

Scene Two The Sitting Room Afternoon November 10, 1882

Empty. Knock. **Williamson** *comes in.*

Williamson Doctor Marx? Doctor Marx?

Where is he?

Coming in behind **Williamson**.

Oh.

Marx Forgive me. I was in Miss Maclaren's kitchen, you know, once again failing to mind my own business.

Williamson Wasn't that rather stretching the terms of your house arrest?

Marx They were jam tarting.

Williamson You like jam tarts?

Marx Our own cook Helene is a masterful maker.

Williamson Marvellous. I'll tell my wife. She's a bit of a wizard herself. What's your preferred filling?

Marx Well. The berries of the Black Forest, you know. But not tasted since my exile for many years.

Williamson Quince?

Marx Too expensive.

Williamson Well. We'll see if we can put that right. I must apologise. I intended to come this morning but there was an emergency that – Well, not an emergency at all, as it

	turned out. Little boy. Staying here with his nanny and her sister. He's a grandson of the Duke of Marlborough.
Marx	Ah. The famous Battle of Blenheim.
Williamson	And Ramillies.
Marx	Malplaquet.
Williamson	And Oudenarde. He has a grand name. Winston Spencer Churchill.
Marx	Poor child. Should you tell me this?
Williamson	No. But he had an interesting gaze. Like yours. We have them all here, you see. The Empress of Austria, even.
Marx	An unhappy woman.
Williamson	And the literati are down the lane at Bonchurch. How have you been?
Marx	Literati?
Williamson	Forty years ago, actually. Dickens. The Swinburnes who lived there. Lord Macaulay.
Marx	The historian.
Williamson	Yes.
Marx	Well.
Williamson	Do I detect disapproval?
Marx	He is like that French fool Michelet.
Williamson	I don't know who that is.

Marx	Another famous supposed historian. He wrote in a style in which it was impossible to tell the truth.

Williamson *is amused but decides not to rise to it.*

Williamson	As I say. How have you been?
Marx	Better.
Williamson	Your sleep?
Marx	Broken but less troubled.
Williamson	Bad dreams?
Marx	No.
Williamson	Pain?
Marx	More of a shortage of breath.
Williamson	And you haven't just sat and brooded.
Marx	No.
Williamson	Excellent. So I must explain about your walks.
Marx	I can walk out?
Williamson	You can.
Marx	The order of release.
Williamson	Indeed. Provided.
Marx	Provided?
Williamson	Well. I'm sure that you've done your homework on our Ventnor climate, and why we have here the National Hospital for Respiratory Diseases.
Marx	The Undercliff, and its particular climate.

Williamson	Yes.
Marx	Which we saw those years ago from the excursion steamer.
Williamson	You would have.
Marx	A geological fault which when it collapsed left a protected coastal strip, and I am not a botanist, you know, but I do notice the range of plant species.
Williamson	Indeed. Imported exotics.
Marx	Did Miss Maclaren tell me that you collect data for a book about this?
Williamson	Well. About the medical aspects. It's not just the mild winters that I'm interested in. My data is about changes in temperature and humidity as one ascends or descends the Undercliff, or as one is nearer to or further from the sea, and the effect of these changes upon respiratory conditions.
Marx	Which relates to my permission to walk?
Williamson	It does.
Marx	Excellent. Please continue.
Williamson	Well. Look out of the windows at Ventnor. It is, I believe, as large an urban area on a landslip as any in Europe.
Marx	Is it safe?
Williamson	More or less.
Marx	More or less.

Williamson	It's honeycombed with natural springs. You can stand in the High Street at dead of night, they say, and hear waters rushing beneath you.
Marx	A marvellous tale to while away the winter, but please come to my walks.
Williamson	Well. Ventnor's streets, are they not, are at widely different heights above the sea, as are the houses on them, and as a patient's disease advances we advise that he or she moves nearer to the sea. The more humid air is kinder. The remainder of a patient's days may be spent with much less trouble and pain.

Marx thinks about it.

Marx	But here, at St Boniface Gardens, we are nearly as high above the sea as is possible.
Williamson	Yes.
Marx	And the effect of the drier air?
Williamson	The effect of the drier air can be to help clear some patient's lungs.
Marx	Thank you.
Williamson	Nevertheless.
Marx	What?
Williamson	I have two recommendations. The first is that when you go out you take with you a respirator.

Marx would interrupt but checks himself.

Marx	If I must. Very well. Go on.
Williamson	The second is that you take a medication in addition to the liniment.
Marx	A second.
Williamson	It will help you at night.

Not much of a response.

> You doubt me? What have I said?

***Marx** knows he must make up his mind.*

Marx	Forgive me. My worries are about the cost. The constant circumstance of my life.

Williamson *waits.*

> Is it a brew? What's in it?

Williamson *has already written the prescription and hands it to **Marx**.*

Marx *reads it.*

> Quinine Desulphuricum. This is new. I have not had this before. The morphine and so on, yes. But not this.

Williamson	It should bring down any tendency to fever.

***Marx** weighs it for a moment.*

> Miss Maclaren can send the maid to the pharmacy, I imagine.

Marx	Thank you. Yes. I trust you. Let us see to it now.

They go out.

Scene Three   The Sitting Room   Afternoon   November 19, 1882

Marx *comes in. He wears his cloak and soft felt hat and is in top spirits.*
But he gives himself a blast on the respirator after climbing the stairs.
*Then his daughter Eleanor, nicknamed **Tussy**, comes in. She is 26,*
tallish, thin, dark, restlessly good-looking.

Tussy	Here, father. Miss Maclaren says someone left this for you. What can it be?

A shopping bag: it contains two pots of jam and a note.

Marx	This is most kind, you know, Eleanor. I discussed jam with Doctor Williamson and he said that his wife makes the most excellent quince and here we are, she has sent me two jars. Keep the bag, she says, its reclamation is an excuse for us to visit.
Tussy	Lovely. You had need of your respirator?
Marx	Where's my little Johnny grandson?
Tussy	With the maid. Two doors up.
Marx	Two doors up?
Tussy	A cat has had kittens.
Marx	Yes, yes. I heard. And look. There is the coach of milord Coghill halted for the third time this week.

Tussy *does not respond.*

                What?

You haven't answered my question.

	Oh. You mean the respirator? I came too quickly up the staircase.

She is not entirely satisfied by this answer.

Marx	My darling Tussy, we have walked when before I could not walk at all. On the Downs. To Bonchurch and the ducks on the pond to amuse little Johnny and almost to the shore. We walked. This is my improvement, you know. The medicines I take act to shorten the transition period up to the point where complete recovery is achieved by fresh air and activity outdoors.
Tussy	Yes.
Marx	I am in sight of myself again. After how many years?
Tussy	I know. Have you met Mrs Williamson?
Marx	What? Oh. No. Not yet. The doctor. A nice young fellow. Nothing priestly about him. No pretence that health is a mystery that laymen cannot understand.
Tussy	So Miss Maclaren confirms.
Marx	Unlike milord Coghill, I suspect.
Tussy	Milord?
Marx	No, no. He is a mister. But he is Chief Medical officer at the hospital, you know, and very good. His hat and boots are very expensive.
Tussy	His boots.

Marx   He has his post and his private business as well, such as the hypochondria of the old lady downstairs.

Tussy   You're an old bear, father, d'you know that?

Marx   She pays him to listen to how ill she is. Twice a week. Three times.

Tussy   How do you know they aren't a pair of Tsarist agents?

Marx   What?

Tussy   I'm joking.

Marx   Tsarist agents are no joke, Tussy.

Tussy   But you could be a conspirator. In your cloak and your slouchy slouch hat you're like a cartoon of a bomb-thrower.

Marx   Through this window, darling, I see the English bourgeois who think themselves so safe. I laugh at their hypocrisy and am bemused, I confess, by their kindness. To hear out a hypochondriac is after all a sort of a good deed.

Tussy   I've met her before. She's frail. She's not hypochondriac at all.

Marx   She goes to the Ventnor sea front every day.

Tussy   Pushed. In a chair with rubber wheels.

Marx   Your high spirits keep me young, Tussy. Stay. Don't go back to London.

Tussy   I must go.

Marx	Must?
Tussy	I've a small part for the play-reading group.
Marx	Small?
Tussy	I think sometimes that if I cannot become an actress I'll go mad.
Marx	I'm stopping you?
Tussy	Yes.
Marx	You always say this. But how?
Tussy	By nothing.
Marx	So?
Tussy	By seeing nothing you don't want to see. By being yourself. You rely on me but you never see me.
Marx	No. No. No. It is true that I stopped you from one thing once. I said no, you must not see this ridiculous Frenchman with ridiculous names.
Tussy	Hyppolite was not ridiculous.
Marx	Hyppolite? Hyppostupid.
Tussy	He loved me.
Marx	A French socialist? Another popinjay rapscallion impostor like those we already suffer? Like that Lafargue your sister Laura married and like your sister Jenny's husband Longuet, a windbag and a bully who hits her I am convinced and -

Tussy	You don't know that.
Marx	Do you want a marriage like theirs?
Tussy	Very well. No. I was young. I didn't know. But -
Marx	Do you want a marriage like your mother's?
Tussy	What?
Marx	I ruined her life. A magnificent woman of discernment and position, and I must steal the fire from the Gods, you know, that is my destiny, but I destroyed her, and now I compare our idealism with those French supposed Socialist tricksters. They believe in a better future, they say, and so they must be morally good. But this does not follow, and I think what have we done? Have we created some new drug of a religion that draws hypocrites as putrefaction draws flies, and justifies the worst in people?
Tussy	But it was beautiful.
Marx	When our ideas have changed the world there will of course be a new morality, but – What?
Tussy	Beautiful. Your life with Mother. The love between you. The courage.

He stops.

It was.

The unsolvable contradiction in his life.

Scene Three 199

	When we went away after she was dead and where was it – Algiers? – Algiers. We sat in that sunlight and remembered her grace, and you cried when you described her wedding day. Her green silk dress and –
Stop.	
Silence.	
He finishes for her.	
Marx	And her garland of pink roses.
Silence.	
	And my book that I dedicate to her not finished, Tussy. The work not finished.
Tussy	No.
Silence.	
	I'd better fetch Johnny.
Gets up.	
Almost gone.	
He calls her back.	
Marx	Tussy.
She checks.	
	You went back to France to help Jennychen in her pregnancy and that was good, but the delivery was hard so you brought your eldest nephew little Johnny to England because it would be some relief and that is good, but –
Should he say it?	

He must.

| | But Tussy, what have you not told me? |

Tussy   Not told you?

Not told me.

| | Nothing. |

Marx   Darling, all the days you have been here you have watched me, to see what I suspected.

Tussy   No.

Marx   No?

Tussy   No. I watched you to see if what you tell me about your health is true or not.

And of course he never has told her all the truth.

Marx   Should I come with you to London?

Tussy   No.

Marx   Should I take Johnny back to France?

Tussy   No. Your recovery is more important.

Marx   But if you go, how can you take part in the play reading?

Tussy   Moor, please get better, and work.

The ongoing dilemma.

Marx   Will you have one of the jars from Mrs Williamson?

Tussy   I'd love to. Thank you. Now I'd better save the kittens from Johnny.

She goes.

He gathers his cloak and slouchy hat, and takes them into the bedroom.

Scene Four   The Sitting Room   Afternoon   December 1882

***Marx** comes in from the bedroom. Books. Letters. His magnifying glass.*
Knock at the door.

Marx   Yes. Who? Come!

It is **Doctor Williamson**.

Ah! My good friend! Welcome.

Williamson   Doctor Marx.

Marx   Fine weather.

Williamson   Are you walking?

Marx   Of course.

Williamson   I've brought you a visitor.

It is **Mrs Williamson**. *A little younger than her husband.*
She has a small muslin-wrapped parcel.

This is Doctor Marx. My wife. Mrs Williamson.

Marx   My dear lady. Do you come to reclaim your shopping bag?

Mrs Williamson   I do. And to meet you. And since Christmas is nearly upon us, to deliver these mince pies.

Marx   Well. I'm not sure that I've ever believed in Christmas, you know, except as a manifestation of our pre-disposition to mythical explanations, but to good cheer let there be no end. Thank you.

Mrs Williamson	And there's nothing to stop us sampling one now, you know.
Marx	Excellent. Three plates?
Williamson	As a matter of fact, two only.
Marx	You don't eat mince pies?
Williamson	Well, as you probably know, a fortnight ago the cook gashed her thumb and I was sent for to stitch it up, so I have to pop downstairs now to snip out my handiwork.
Marx	I trust that you will subject your blade to the flame.
Williamson	Well remembered. I will. And leave you with Mrs Williamson.
Marx	Unchaperoned?
Williamson	I thought that my top hat could do that.
Marx	Chaperone.
Williamson *taps it.*	
Williamson	Of course. Shan't be long.
He goes.	
Marx	What a resourceful young fellow.
Mrs Williamson	Isn't he? Are you all right?
Marx	Recovering.
Mrs Williamson	Yes. Good. He talks about you, you see, and I'm as curious as a cat, and have all sorts of questions.

Marx	About the philosophy of historical change?
Mrs Williamson	Good Lord, no. Shall we take a bite?

They unwrap the muslin.

And chew.

Appreciatively.

Mrs Williamson	Mm....
Marx	Wunderbar.
Mrs Williamson	My questions are about these things of which a non-conformist clergyman's daughter such as myself is too pure to have knowledge.
Marx	When you say "pure", do you imply protected?
Mrs Williamson	Very good. Yes. I must, mustn't I?
Marx	I think so.
Mrs Williamson	So it's true that your intimates call you Moor?
Marx	Moor. Yes.
Mrs Williamson	Why?
Marx	Because I'm dark and very bearish.
Mrs Williamson	Moors aren't actually bears, though, are they?
Marx	No.
Mrs Williamson	But I see the point.

Marx	Thank you. And I am called Moor because to people we like we give nicknames.
Mrs Williamson	We?
Marx	My wife and – My late wife and – The family. My sons who died were called Fawkesy, because he was born on your Firework Day, and Colonel Monsch, and Laura is Hottentot, and Jenny Jennychen, and Eleanor is Tussy.
Mrs Williamson	Tussy?
Marx	To rhyme with Pussycat.
Mrs Williamson	Of course.
Marx	And Mr Engels is General.
Mrs Williamson	What would you call me? If you liked me, that is.
Marx	Pie Lady.
Mrs Williamson	Very good. Would I be taking pies to market?
Marx	No. To Hans Röckle's shop.
Mrs Williamson	Hans Röckle?
Marx	A magician.
Mrs Williamson	In Germany?
Marx	He has a shop.
Mrs Williamson	Of course.
Marx	It is full of wooden toys.
Mrs Williamson	Models?

Marx	Men. Women. Dwarves. Kings. Queens. Workmen. Masters. Birds. Tables. Chairs. Boxes. Carriages.
Mrs Williamson	Is Hans real?
Marx	I invented him. And the adventures of the toys. To amuse the children.
Mrs Williamson	Marvellous.
Marx	What other things?
Mrs Williamson	The rest of these pies must be saved for Christmas. What?

He lets her return to it herself.

> Oh. Sorry. Yes. Things to ask you about. Well –

Deep breath.

Smile.

Then she plunges in.

> What was it like when you were arrested?

Marx Ah. Now that is a good question, you know, because like any experience an arrest can depend on the circumstances. In France my arrest was – Well, it is no secret that I suspect the French. I have the most despicable French sons-in-law and – I have learned with age not to explode. Would you believe that when I was young I would write a hundred pages of venomous polemic in reply to Utopian charlatans who imagined they understood me?

Mrs Williamson I would believe.

Marx Today I ignore pinpricks.

Mrs Williamson So do I. But I'm a girl, of course.

Marx That observation itself shows how much is wrong with the world.

Mrs Williamson If you'd asked me, I'd have said that I thought that you'd like the French. I mean, didn't they invent revolutions?

About to answer.

Thinks better of it.

Marx Shall we confine ourselves to my arrests?

Mrs Williamson Probably a jolly good idea.

Marx The Prussian arrest was as efficient as one would expect, and the Belgian unpleasant.

Mrs Williamson Were they violent?

Marx They expelled us. So we came to England. No. The Belgians were vulgar, somehow. Very coarse. Unsubtle.

Mrs Williamson Well. I went to Ostend once, and Flemish is a very harsh language.

Marx I agree with you. It is. The English arrest was of course the most ludicrous.

Mrs Williamson Oh. I thought that we extended our tolerance.

Marx In political matters of course. Although I was refused citizenship. But the arrest was not political.

Mrs Williamson	Really?
Marx	No, no. We were poor, you know. Very untidy. Rickety furniture. Very old clothes. Then my wife came into a modest inheritance which included historic family silver. This was convenient, because as we continued to be poor we could continue to pawn candlesticks and table pieces and so forth, and one day I went to do so and was arrested.
Mrs Williamson	Why?
Marx	Because a person of such disreputable appearance but in possession of such valuable pieces, it was assumed, could only be a burglar.
Mrs Williamson	Of course. What happened?
Marx	My wife was sent for, but again, how could a woman in such old clothes possibly be a baroness?
Mrs Williamson	Easily. By her manner.
Marx	Exactly. A senior officer was summoned and knew it at once.
Mrs Williamson	Marvellous.
Marx	But they had not read me as a scholar.
Mrs Williamson	What's that, they would enquire.
Marx	As my daughter Tussy says, Mrs Williamson, I have identified the importance of the class war and the ways in which it drives historical change,

	but at the same time managed to know very little about you English.
Mrs Williamson	If it's true, how is that?
Marx	Because I met so few. I think. Yes. That must be why.
Mrs Williamson	But you've lived here for what? Thirty odd years?
Marx	But who have I met? My family and other political refugees. Other Germans for the most part. My days were in the British Museum Library, or sleeping off hangovers.
Mrs Williamson	Hangovers.
Marx	Do the non-conformist chapels not recognise hangovers?
Mrs Williamson	Not as everyday acquaintances, no.
Marx	Yet a hangover was at the end of the one time I deserved to be arrested.
Mrs Williamson	In England?
Marx	London. I was with a band of German socialists, you know, most of us renting in Soho, and we decided one evening to walk the Tottenham Court Road, and to have a glass of beer in every licensed premises between Oxford Street and the Hampstead Road.
Mrs Williamson	How many was that?
Marx	Eighteen.
Mrs Williamson	Eighteen pubs?

Marx	Yes.
Mrs Williamson	What happened?
Marx	In the last hostelry there was an explosive argument, you know, between ourselves and English I suppose medical students or night doctors about the superiority of German culture. We were chased out.
Mrs Williamson	Quite right.
Marx	It was two a.m.
Mrs Williamson	Oh, dear.
Marx	We threw stones at the street lamps, and extinguished several.
Mrs Williamson	Police whistles?
Marx	Police whistles. A chase. But we were conspirators, Mrs Williamson, and we knew the back alleys.
Mrs Williamson	You escaped.
Marx	We did.
Mrs Williamson	But with later hangovers.

With hangovers, says his body language.

And it reminds him of something sad.

For which she waits.

Marx	And worse. Our son Fawkesy died in Soho. Our poverty. We hated the place. We left. Never paid what we owed, or – Forgive me. This should be minced pies merriment, no?

Mrs Williamson	Without sorrow there might never be merriment.

He appreciates this.

Marx	Do you enjoy charades?
Mrs Williamson	I do. They're almost as good as new clothes.
Marx	We played all those games, you see. Children and dogs most excited. Rum Crambo. Charades. Many puzzles.
Mrs Williamson	Rum?
Marx	Correct. Dumb.
Mrs Williamson	I think so.
Marx	And the charades we did in all our languages.
Mrs Williamson	Golly. Do show me.
Marx	Well. The answer would be English. But the clues might be German or French or Italian or Latin or – Mr Engels was perverse once, and displayed his limited knowledge of Serbo-Croat.
Mrs Williamson	Can we have a go?
Marx	Why not?
Mrs Williamson	But don't start me off with something complicated.
Marx	I promise. Let me see. Yes. This is basic.

He gets up to act out the charade.

All in dumb show.

Number of fingers to indicate the syllable count.
Gestures to say correct guess or not.
He starts off to show the whole world.
Hands pointed and then spread out above his head.

Mrs Williamson That's the whole word?

Thumbs up.

     Arrowhead.

No. No.

     In that case.

Wait.

One.

Despondence.

Slumped in evident pain.

     Glum.

No.

     Down.

No.

More violent motions.

     Convulsions.

No.

     Sorry. One syllable at a time. What? What?

Heaving.

     Vomit.

No.

                Vom. Surely not?

No.

                It.

No.

Even more horrible.

                Throw.

No.

                Sick!

Yes.

                Hooray!

Now wait.

Number two.

Swooning.

Reeling.

Heavy breathing.

                Reel.

No.

                Room. Sickroom. No.

No.

Heart on heart.

Protestations.

                No. I can't think of a – Yes. Amour.

Yes.

                Sycamore.

Yes.

        Part English. Part French. I get it.

Marx   Well done.

Mrs Williamson   It's not made you cough, has it?

Up to a point.

But better.

Don't worry.

        Permission to try, then?

Marx   Please.

This time she stands.

Thinks.

Then she's got it.

Ready.

This is the whole word.

Sitting.

Very upright.

Then a gesture to graciously acknowledge respect.

Then standing.

Watching.

Then swooping forward.

Catching something in the teeth.

Shaking and worrying something.

        A very wet dog.

No.

Mrs Williamson And don't be silly.

Wait.

This is the first syllable.

*Miming picking up something and putting it on **Marx's** head.*

Marx Crown.

No.

Then she bows.

King!

Thumbs up! Yes!
Now the second syllable.
She mimes waiting and watching.
With something held out in front of her.
Then sudden activity.

Angle!

No.

No. The other word.

Reeling in.

Fisher.

Yes.

Kingfisher.

Mrs Williamson Yes.

Marx Excellent.

Mrs Williamson I thought of doing Boniface. Face being French, of course. But I couldn't in the instant think of a mime for Boni.

Marx	Perhaps bow and knee.
Mrs Williamson	Brilliant. Or –

She mimes with one hand the hat and with the other the hand stuck in the coat.

He gets it.

Marx	Napoleon?
Mrs Williamson	Bonaparte. Boney. Or would that be very marginally cheating?
Marx	There would be a ruling by the committee.
Mrs Williamson	Yes.
Marx	Who is this St Boniface anyway?
Mrs Williamson	I believe that he converted many of the Germans.
Marx	Then he has much to answer for.
Mrs Williamson	May I ask a very impertinent question?
Marx	Please.
Mrs Williamson	Are you aware that your jacket is mis-buttoned?
Marx	Oh. Thank you.

He corrects it.

	I am, of course, although I pretend not to be, short-sighted.
Mrs Williamson	But you read and write entire libraries, my husband says.
Marx	With a magnifying glass.
Mrs Williamson	Very professional.

Marx	I have still more than once, in London, gone out for a walk and returned to the wrong front door.
Mrs Williamson	Well, that could be an adventure, couldn't it? One of your magician's wooden toys walks around Bonchurch, and is surprised by where he is.
Marx	Somehow, their stories were always the same.
Mrs Williamson	How?
Marx	Hans Röckle was so poor, you know, that he had always to sell his toys to the Devil. But they always came back, somehow, in the evening, to the shop.
Mrs Williamson	I don't know whether that's sad or not.

Neither does he, quite.

She is still on her feet, of course, and looking out.

	Like this, you see. Is this sad?
Marx	What?
Mrs Williamson	This mist, that comes up from the sea into the town.
Marx	It is what our emotions make of it.
Mrs Williamson	Sad when we ourselves are sad?
Marx	Yes. And there is a reason why we say the fog of war.
Mrs Williamson	The smoke of the guns, surely.
Marx	Our hatreds, which blind our eyes.

Scene Four

Mrs Williamson   Actually, my husband said not to mention politics. Your recovery depends on calm, he said.

Marx   After mince pies and charades I am very calm.

Mrs Williamson   In that case, is it true that you believe that everything can be changed and made perfect?

Marx   Well, we are marvellous creatures, you know, but society can alienate us, you know, from who we are and what we could be.

Mrs Williamson   What we could be.

Marx   Yes.

Mrs Williamson   And to find ourselves, what must we do?

Marx   Be sensible.

Mrs Williamson   Who's to say what that is?

Marx   It can be explained, I believe.

She would ask more.

But should she?

Would it agitate him?

   I observe that you do not wish to agitate me.

Mrs Williamson   No.

Marx   Thank you. My next answer would be that it may be a question of what makes us selfish.

Mrs Williamson   What does?

Marx	I am not convinced, you see, that we must be so forever.
Mrs Williamson	Well, my father preached sermons about that.
Marx	He looked for what is supposed to be God's way, I imagine. I look to rationality. If we accept what must happen we can develop.

She starts to speak but stops.

	This confuses you?
Mrs Williamson	No, but people who oppose God are called sinners, and although one struggles to comprehend an actual hell, they are punished.
Marx	Supposedly.
Mrs Williamson	What would happen to people who opposed you?
Marx	Opposed me? The world opposes me.
Mrs Williamson	What I mean is that if property is theft, as my husband says you think it is, would you take it away from people? And how would they respond? Or would they have had their heads cut off, like those people in the French Revolution?

He looks. But she was not criticising him.

Mrs Williamson	I'm sorry. Flippant. But do you see what worries me?

Marx	Of course. What, in our circumstances, you wonder, is to be the basis of morality?
Mrs Williamson	Our circumstances?
Marx	A future without God.
Mrs Williamson	Is that how one should think of life now?
Marx	Mrs Williamson, these are the very battles of our German philosophy. For example, can evil as it is called be abolished?
Mrs Williamson	My father would have said – I'm not sure what he'd say.
Marx	It is my life's struggle to find a way through these mists. Can you understand?
Mrs Williamson	Of course. You're one of the prophets.

Doctor Williamson *is there.*

Williamson	Profits? Aren't they what you wag your finger against, Doctor Marx?
Marx	Your husband is a humorist, you know, like knowing that this hat would be such an excellent chaperone. How is the cook?
Williamson	Fortunate. She has almost no loss of function.

Indicates a thumb twiddle.

Marx	Good. I must thank you, Mrs Williamson. It has been a true pleasure.
Mrs Williamson	Mutual.

Marx   Might I escort you to the top of the staircase?

They go out.

Scene Five   The Sitting Room   Morning   January 6, 1883

This is before breakfast, even. An emergency call out. ***Williamson*** *comes from the bedroom.*

Williamson   I think that on balance you should get up, yes. You might find it easier to be upright, and let the morphine work.

What more can he say or do?

But he gathers himself. The professional manner.

Marx *appears. Dressing gown. He looks very shaken.*

Marx   Can it be true? That mental anguish does touch the movements of the mucus?

Williamson   There is no good data either way, but yes. It would seem that it can.

Marx *starts to explain more.*

                            Doctor Marx. Please. No speech. I understand you. Can you answer my questions with a nod or a shake of the head?

Nod.

                            Have you been bringing up mucus all week?

Nod.

    Has there been blood in it?

Neither a nod nor a shake.

    Sometimes?

Nod.

    Big splotches, or threads?

Midway again.

    Threads.

Nod.

    All week?

Shake.

    Last night?

Marx   I coughed so much that I was afraid I would suffocate.

Williamson   What did you do?

Marx   Spoonfuls of water.

Williamson   That was effective?

Wheezing breath instead of speech.

    Rest a moment.

They both wait.

Marx   I awake. Where am I? Choking in mucus. I'm in terror. I think I will die. Then I think this is impossible. How can I die tonight? How can I die if I'm able to think that I'm dying? It will be another night. Or day. In the future.

Williamson   I understand.

Marx   You don't.

Williamson   Then tell me. But calmly.

Marx   I need to expel rage like the mucus.

Then go ahead. But more calmly.

>Exiles of my age are from the failed revolutions of 1848. Most had bourgeois ideals. They wanted a share of the spoils, not transformation. My sons-in-law are from the Paris Commune of 1870 – a more proletarian struggle. But for whatever reason they are posturers. Vain bullies and chance-takers. At least when they were in London we could see our daughters and help them. Then a new French government declared an amnesty, and Communards were able to return to France, which our sons-in-law did and took our daughters with them and – We were told nothing and if we visited were accused of interference even by the girls and when Tussy returns from a visit she tells nothing and –

Williamson *waits.*

>Yesterday came a letter from the scoundrel Lafargue, the husband of our daughter Laura, about her sister our daughter Jenny who is married to the windbag editor Longuet –

*Again **Williamson** has to wait.*

> Jenny's life was difficult and her pregnancies were hell. And Lafargue writes not from duty or compassion, you understand, but to make problems – I was not told anything before.

Williamson *hesitates.*

Williamson	Did you disagree with the husbands politically?
Marx	It is they who went against me.
Williamson	What have you told them about your own ailments?

***Marx** would make a vigorous reply but checks.*

Marx Good. Thank you. The points are taken. The rebuke is taken. But I said little so as not to agitate them. After all, I will recover my strength, and continue my work. Lafargue's news was that Jenny has cancer of the bladder, and no time at all to live.

Williamson *absorbs this. Then –*

Williamson Which news, of course, was the cause of your episode in the night.

Marx Yes.

Williamson Yes.

They both consider it.

Marx Is it painful?

Williamson Cancer of the bladder?

Marx	Yes.
Williamson	As you know, there is always the morphine.
Marx	Which does not always soothe my own spasms.
Williamson	Would you want me to increase the dosage?

No. That's not it.

Marx	But it will be for our Jenny disgusting, no?
Williamson	I'm sure that she receives the best of care.
Marx	Wrecked lives, you know. Wrecked by my what I call refusal to compromise. Is that why they tell me nothing?
Williamson	My only data, so to speak, is their evident reverence for you.
Marx	The bedside manner. Very good.

Both wryly accept it.

	It is ironic, but I did once apply for regular paid work in England, you know.
Williamson	Really?
Marx	To be a clerk in the offices of a railway company.
Williamson	What happened?
Marx	I was rejected.
Williamson	Why?

Marx	The illegibility of my handwriting.
Williamson	Crikey.
Marx	We must not laugh. I do not want to laugh.

They manage not to laugh.

Just about.

And **Williamson** *has a follow-up point.*

Williamson	But hasn't writing been the point of your life?
Marx	It has: and two thirds of my fundamental book still to be revised.
Williamson	What's it called?
Marx	Das Kapital.
Williamson	It's in German.
Marx	Of course.
Williamson	What I meant, actually, was: if your writing's so poor, what about editors and typesetters?
Marx	My wife copied everything in her immaculate gentlewoman's copperplate.

Of course, acknowledges **Williamson**. *Of course.*

Williamson	Would she have liked Ventnor, d'you think?
Marx	She liked what she saw from the pleasure steamer.
Williamson	Have you walked down to Bonchurch shore yet?

Marx	Not as far as the shore itself.
Williamson	One day soon, then, maybe.
Marx	Yes.

Another reflective little silence.

Williamson	If you'd been there in 1588 you'd have seen the Spanish Armada.
Marx	This I realised already from the books, you know.
Williamson	And it's where Dickens and Swinburne played scratch cricket.
Marx	The English Cricket.
Williamson	Baffling?
Marx	Baffling.

They ponder this.

	And milord Coghill and the ancient hypochondriac. This is also a good story, no?
Williamson	I never hear a word about a senior colleague.
Marx	Of course. I apologise.

Wants to laugh. Manages not to.

Williamson *observes this. Then –*

Williamson	You seem pretty stable now, actually.
Marx	The morphine.
Williamson	Are you all right if I leave you?
Marx	I am. It is, despite everything, my duty.

Williamson	To prepare for your work.
Marx	My work.

Williamson *understands.*

He gathers his things.

Marx	This call was early, good Doctor. Did you miss breakfast?
Williamson	I can just nip back home for an egg.

Marx smiles and nods.

Williamson *smiles.*

And goes.

Marx sits for a moment. Then to the bedroom.

Scene Six   The Sitting Room   Midday   11 January 1883

*Marx comes out to meet **Tussy** as she bursts into the room. She has travelled.*

Marx	Tussy? You came back? You never warned me. Why? What – ?

She does not know what to say.

	No need to tell. I can see. Our Jennychen is dead.

Yes. Yes she is.

	When did you hear?
Tussy	By telegram. I came at once.
Marx	Then we must return at once.
Tussy	What?

Marx	To London: and you to France: we cannot leave the children with their absurd father.
Tussy	Her end was peaceful, the telegram said.
Marx	They are all liars, Tussy, and we must act as we see fit.
Tussy	Moor, why can it not occur to you that they are not grand villains but merely ordinary and confused people?
Marx	You need to wash and have some refreshments and then we will go to the railway station.
Tussy	My entire life is spent upon other people and not myself.
Marx	You don't want to go?
Tussy	Of course I want to go. It makes me weep, but of course I want to go.
Marx	No more weeping, my darling. Action. The struggle.
Tussy	Moor: are you yourself?
Marx	Thanks to the St Boniface Gardens and the help I have received I will be myself. Soon. Again. And work. Who cares if everything that we socialists have hoped for is not achieved at once? Perhaps everything at once was the delusion of Robespierre, you know. What we want is steps to better things and – Painless.
Tussy	Yes.
Marx	They said painless.

Tussy	Yes.
Marx	Do you believe them?
Tussy	I don't know. Please don't torture me anymore.
Marx	You will be an actress. I promise. Our sorrows will end.
Tussy	Are you untidy like this all day?
Marx	Where's my reading glass? What's the date?
Tussy	January Eleven 1883.
Marx	We must pay Miss Maclaren and I need to write to Doctor Williamson to send his account to London and I will sign the photograph for his wife and –

Silence.

In a hundred years, who will know the lilt of our Jenny's voice?

Silence.

Tussy	Can I have my little wash, now, Moor, after the journey?
Marx	Of course. And if I dress and gather my things and you ask the maid to call a cab and – Painless, they said.
Tussy	Yes.

Silence. They have too much and nothing to say.

Marx	And Tussy.
Tussy	What?

Marx Courage.

Nod. She goes to call the cab and he to dress.

Music has carried us through the play – the dark side of Nineteenth century German Romanticism – and now the gods cross into Valhalla perhaps as in ...

The Epilogue

Mrs Williamson *has come out of their house to greet her returning husband.*

Mrs Williamson	James, darling. Welcome back. How was smoky London?
Williamson	I brought you this newspaper.
Mrs Williamson	What?
Williamson	Sad news, sweetheart.

He proffers the newspaper folded at the page.

No, says her head-shake and gesture. You read it.

So he does.

"March 15 1883. The death is announced of Doctor Karl Marx, the German Socialist. He had lived to see the portions of his theories which once terrified Emperors and Chancellors die out..." And so on and so forth... "English working men would not care to be identified with these principles..."

	The Daily News. I think there was a paragraph in The Times.
Mrs Williamson	Wooden toys…
Williamson	What?
Mrs Williamson	Extraordinary man.
Williamson	Yes.
Mrs Williamson	I do think about what he said to me…

Then…

Williamson	He had this massive abscess on the lung.
Mrs Williamson	Which you detected?
Williamson	Almost at once.
Mrs Williamson	And knew that he would die.

No reply.

But you never told him.

No reply.

Sorry. Shouldn't ask.

Williamson	I'm peckish, actually. Can we go in?
Mrs Williamson	Out of the sea mist. Yes. And I can give you a hug and tell you my news.
Williamson	What?
Mrs Williamson	Come on.

They go in. There's music.

The End of the Play

www.ingramcontent.com/pod-product-compliance
Lightning Source LLC
LaVergne TN
LVHW041613070426
835507LV00008B/207